INWARDBOUND:

Mindfulness as an Executive Capability

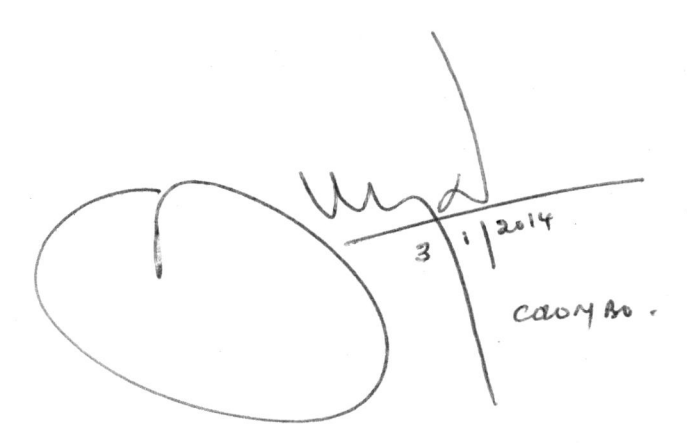

DEEPAL SOORIYAARACHCHI (Deepal Soori)
FCIM (UK) Chartered Marketer, MBA (Sri J). MSLIM

When Deepal took an early retirement from corporate life he was the Managing Director of Aviva Insurance, Sri Lanka operation. He started his career as a clerk in a shop and rose to become the CEO of a blue chip corporate. Chartered Marketer by Profession Deepal experimented with how ancient wisdom of the East, particularly the teachings of Buddhism, can be amalgamated with the business world of today. *Inwardbound* is a result of his lifelong experiment of bringing Mindfulness to the work of business leadership. He has eleven publications to his credit, and offers Executive Development consultancy services.

INWARDBOUND:

Mindfulness as an Executive Capability

Deepal Soori

INWARDBOUND:

Mindfulness as an Executive Capability

Olympia Publishers
London

www.olympiapublishers.com
OLYMPIA PAPERBACK EDITION

Copyright © Deepal Sooriyaarachchi 2012

The right of Deepal Sooriyaarachchi to be identified as author of this work has been asserted in accordance with sections 77 and 78 of the Copyright, Designs and Patents Act 1988.

All Rights Reserved

No reproduction, copy or transmission of this publication may be made without written permission.
No paragraph of this publication may be reproduced, copied or transmitted save with the written permission of the publisher, or in accordance with the provisions of the Copyright Act 1956 (as amended).

Any person who commits any unauthorised act in relation to this publication may be liable to criminal prosecution and civil claims for damage.

A CIP catalogue record for this title is available from the British Library.

ISBN: 978-1-84897-187-5

First Published in 2012

Olympia Publishers
60 Cannon Street
London
EC4N 6NP

Printed in Great Britain

To my wife Sunethra

For being my best friend in my life's journey

To have credibility, ideally, a preacher should also be a practitioner. Deepal is indeed someone who has tested the techniques he is espousing – he walks the talk! With several examples that are easy to understand and experience, he reinforces his message on the need to be mindful. He also demonstrates the power of the "Why" over "What" – when dealing with stressful situations. Even if you grasp just 25% of his message, you will see an enormous change in your life. As a specialist in the decision-making arena, I found his insights extremely valuable.

Errol Wirasinghe, Ph.D.
Author, "The Art of Making Decisions"
Developer of the XpertUS Decision Support System

Self-Awareness is a key component of Emotional Intelligence
(Daniel Goleman) and a critical capability for today's successful executive.

Mindfulness is one approach to increase self-awareness. In today's world where speed continues to accelerate and executives are called upon to do "more with less", it is easy to lose sight of the "self" as a "tool". Deepal defines mindfulness and offers simple exercises to develop this capability, as well as examples of how to apply it using "real work" gained from his many years as a senior executive. He shares the power of this in his own personal and executive life. This is a short, practical guide for any executive who wants to travel "inward" from someone who has lived the daily pressures of executive life. Our impact in life may have as much to do with our "being" as with our "doing".

**Dr. Lynne De Lay,
Leadership Coach & Coaching Supervisor, USA.**

Deepal embarks on a journey we often take on reverse! Our typical thinking patterns are outward-bound. They are centred around that which is outside of us. Our focus is on the outside. Deepal's book, *Inwardbound* is essentially about a journey we ought to take on the inside. This journey of self-discovery of being rather than having and doing is well narrated by the author with a sense of clarity that is possible from one who has actually taken the journey within. Read it. Reflect on it. And you will be richer by the discovery of one you ought to know very well inside-out yourself.

Prof. Uditha Liyanage
Director
**Post Graduate Institute of Management,
University of Sri Jayewardenepura, Sri Lanka**

Introduction

Inwardbound is an intriguing value proposition for jaded western skeptics who work too much. Deepal argues that self-awareness or mindfulness is often missing and when it's missing, life and work are less fulfilling and less effective. I've seen Deepal use these concepts with line executives and witnessed the shift in awareness that results in clearer thinking and better choices. Deepal brings a unique combination of senior executive and eastern mystic with a strong sense of humour to his writing and to his consulting. Read this book. It's fun and it's good for you.

Norm Smallwood
Co founder of the RBL Group and co-author of Leadership Code, Results Based Leadership, and Leadership Brand with Dave Ulrich

Alarm goes… jump out of bed.
Already late for the early morning call conference to speak with business partners across the globe before offices close for the day.
No time to have breakfast, grab a coffee.
A quick hug to the kid rushing to school with the wife who is on her way to work.
Finish the call. Now so many things on the agenda for follow up.
Phone rings again … rush out of shower.
Speed up to office beating traffic…tension builds up.
Traffic lights… why does the red stay for so long?
Waiting for the change … check SMS and mail on BlackBerry.
Phone on hands-off mode – urgent instructions to the PA in office… "will be there just in time for the meeting".
Thinking of the game plan for the tough negotiation ahead.
Luncheon meeting… It was only last week decided to have a low calorie diet but business lunches are far from it.
After lunch have to talk to a long-standing employee – a long-standing friend and loyal employee but now redundant as the function is outsourced.
Oh! the inbox is full with messages urgent and important … ``how the hell can I prioritize?''
Terrible headache… swallow a tablet…
The annual check-up is overdue…get the secretary to fix it for the next week…"oh no – have to fly out".
Bloomberg news flash… market dips so does the share price … end of the week meeting with investors.
Check the diary… evening professional institute presentation… "it's not ready yet"… a call from the organisers – they want the slides sent early.
Phone rings…it's the Business Editor from the local newspaper.

Getting ready to leave office, a call from your son. "Dad – aren't you coming to our school play this evening. I am playing the main role" ... "Oh no! Why did I accept the speaking engagement?"
Juggling with all this just makes it to the play – it was just about to be over.
Take the family for dinner – still on the way home... the phone rings so many times while at dinner.
A set of documents that must be completed before the day begins tomorrow.
A mug of hot coffee ... open the laptop.

Sounds familiar?

Contents

1 Let go of baggage 23
2 What is mindfulness? 25
3 A thought about slowing down 29
4 REACTION vs RESPONSE 30
5 WHY instead of WHAT 34
6 Choose a Practice that suits you 37
Practice 1 Drink your morning cup of tea/coffee as if it is done for the first time in life 38
Practice 2 Eating as a Practice to improve mindfulness 41
Practice 3 Let us learn to walk 43
Practice 4 Shower in the present moment 45
Practice 5 Get dressed mindfully 48
Practice 6 Driving mindfully is a pleasure 49
Practice 7 A few minutes in the garden 51
Practice 8 Get close to nature 53
Practice 9 Ten Direction Look* 54
Practice 10 Cooking in the Present Moment 55
Practice 11 Washing in the Present 56
Practice 12 Music you listen to now 57
Practice 13 Breath our best friend 58
Practice 14 Travelling – moments to perfect the practice ... 63
Practice 15 Practice in the Shopping Mall 65
Practice 16 Art of relaxation 66
Practice 17 Stretch 69
Practice 18 Close Windows before sleep 70
Practice 19 Silence 72
Practice 20 Start slow to drive fast 73

7 Living Mindfully 75
8 Name it to Miss it 80
9 The biggest noise 83
10 The finger and the moon 86
11 Can we really listen? 89
12 Listening is speaking 92
13 Don't waste the arrow 95
14 Dreaming, Day dreaming and Thinking 99
15 Being alone and feeling lonely 102
16 To be alone is a skill 105
17 The Paradigm of "I" 108
18 Is your identity in tact? 111
19 Check the meter before the crash 114
20 Respect and Recognition – handle with care 117
21 'When I feel smaller' 122
22 Is appreciation a skill? 124
23 Who made me unhappy? 127
24 Plug and play Friendships 130
25 Diary and the family 134
26 Which Part of Life? 137
27 Paying Forward instead of Paying Back 140
28 The glass is half full 145
29 Formula to Fail 148
30 The art of giving 154
31 Prisoners of Food 157
32 Examination before the lesson 160
33 Responsibility and Accountability 163
34 Trust as an instinct 166
35 Will you worship the computer? 169
36 Deciding to decide 172
 In Summary 175
37 Post script 177

1

Let go of baggage

In this highly demanding environment, to be effective you need to be in control. To be in control you need to know what goes on here and now. To know what goes on you need to be aware. To be aware you need to be mindful. When you are mindful you have a state of mind that is alert. An alert mind is one that is in command – like the mind of a learner driver. When you were first behind the wheel every single movement needed your attention. When you see your child taking her first ride on the bike without guard wheels you are in total attention, alert to see what happens next. If you ever have walked on a rope or a narrow log to cross a stream, then your mind was in the state of being mindful and aware. Being able to maintain such a state of mind is a skill that can be developed, just as you develop the skill of driving. Once you master the art of driving, you don't think of every move. It happens automatically. The trainers call this 'Unconscious Competency' state. Similarly, when we develop the skill of being mindful we become aware of what goes on right now. Once we know, we are in charge.

Once in charge we can Respond by making a choice instead of just Reacting. Most reactions are habitual.

Once we are aware we can choose to let go of things that are not important right now. We can unload the burden of life for a few seconds, regain strength and carry on again.

Have you ever carried a heavy bag or a parcel? When you started the walk, you never felt it to be that heavy. But a few meters and a few minutes later you begin to realize the weight. You change it from one hand to the other – you might even put it on the ground for a few minutes and carry it again.

Here is a simple exercise. Take a little book, hold it in your stretched hand for some time. You will begin to feel the weight and the hand will begin to ache. The longer you hold it, the greater the pain. The solution is simple, just drop it on the ground for a few minutes and you will be able to pick it up again.

Most of the time, we carry worries in our mind. They are from the past and are invariably linked either to things we have done or things we could not do. The reality is that there is very little we can do about the past. We are also anxious about the future. The future is yet to come – so we can do very little except being prepared. This state of anxiousness builds up stress. Being aware of this state of mind, meaning being mindful, provides that sense of being in charge. It is like keeping the weight on the ground before picking it up again.

2

What is mindfulness?

It is not about "a mind full of things". Well most of the time our minds are full of thoughts. Come to think of it most of these thoughts are either about the future or about the past. But mindfulness is about being able to know what goes on in your mind at present – right now. But it is interesting to know that thoughts come in sequence one after the other. This happens so fast that we cannot even notice it happening unless we really slow down.

For instance, as you read this sentence you may suddenly remember something related to this topic or something completely unrelated. Maybe about some work you were doing yesterday. Then your present thought changes to the thought about the work you did yesterday. The moment you realize it, then you have the thought of awareness – that "it is a thought of knowing" it is different from the previous thought. So in the initial stages of the development of this skill you begin to notice the immediately preceding thought. But if the topic that you are thinking is stronger than the thought of awareness, then it can come back.

Don't worry – it is fun when you start observing this mind game. It is like learning a new language or a craft.

Once you are aware of what goes on in your mind you can take charge.

You have learnt from your childhood the advice – "when you get angry count up to ten before doing or saying anything." But most of the time we realize that we were angry long after action was taken. Developing mindfulness to become aware will help us realize that we are losing our temper as it happens so that we can decide how to respond. Otherwise, the natural tendency is to react through habit.

The other important aspect of developing the ability to become aware of the current mental status is being able to understand the real motives of our own actions. We become more sensitive to our own likes, dislikes, and emotions. This reduces our inner conflicts helping our mental health in the long term. Otherwise, we suppress our emotions without really being aware of them. They then start to grow as pent up emotions to erupt at unexpected moments or cause physical or psychological disorders.

Mindfulness gives us the skill to become aware when the mental loads we carry are too heavy. When we weigh our bags before air travel we know what to leave behind, to pack tight and pack light. Similarly, mindfulness helps us to become aware when the emotional loads are too heavy so we can take stock to let go of things that really bother us.

It is interesting to note how we cling on to thoughts that make us unhappy, like a thought about a person who has done wrong to us. We carry that person in our mind the way we used to carry the loved one in our mind during our courting days. It is the habit formed by the latter – to continue thoughts of pleasure, make us harbour thoughts about the wrongdoer also throughout the day. Once we develop the skill of becoming aware of what we are doing, we can choose not to think about that person in an emotional way. We learn to let go of those thoughts that build emotional pressures.

In some Asian countries hunters use a simple trick to capture monkeys. They make a hole in a coconut that is small so that a monkey can reach inside only by squeezing the hand. Inside the coconut they place peanuts. The monkey reaches for peanuts, grabs a few and closes the fist but fails to pull the hand out with the closed fist. It cannot figure out that by letting go of the peanuts that it can pull the hand out. Eventually the hunters capture the monkey.

To be free the monkey has to let go of the handful of peanuts. This is exactly what happens to us. Only if we let go of the painful thought we can be free from the suffering, so there is space to resolve or take action about the true issue.

Being aware gives us a capability to operate from a different platform that is free from unnecessary baggage.

How do we develop this skill of mindfulness?

Well, like any other skill, we also learn this in a step-by step-way. Once mastered, it is like cycling. It is going to be with you.

How long does it take to develop the skill?

Don't have time targets. You have enough time targets already. This is a natural capability you already have. You are going to rediscover it and fine-tune it. Like any other skill it is all about practicing. Once you start practice it is going to be with you throughout your life.

How do you develop the skill?

Unlike other skill developments, don't be very serious. Make learning this skill fun; after all you learn this to be free!

Don't have a rigid target to be perfect. You have enough of such goals already. The practice itself is the goal. The hen does not check the time but she just sits on her eggs until they hatch. Just because you are in a hurry you cannot cause a flower to bloom. What you can do is water, and look after the plant. Blooming is part of the nature. Similarly, being mindful is a natural capability. You keep practicing and you will realize it has an impact on you. That is all.

If you have learned or heard anything about mindfulness and awareness leave them behind for a while.

You probably have heard this is linked to meditation. If it is in the context of developing one's mind then it is true. Otherwise, forget any other connotations.

You are going to learn to observe some mundane things slowly, very slowly to pick up the art of becoming aware. Once you get the hang of it you can apply it to any phenomena in life and you will discover your own speed and the path.

3

A thought about slowing down

You walk past the trees along the path every day. You hardly notice them unless one day you find a tree is missing.

But if you slow down you may notice the trees, the branches, the tender leaves, the mature ones, the dying ones and those on the ground.

Go closer and you can get a much clearer view of a leaf – all the patterns and the shades, and the tiny insects that live on it.

This is exactly what happens to us in life.

We are kept so busy with all that happens; it is so routine to us. Not being busy seems to be so unusual. The result of this 'busy-ness' is that we fail to notice not only the beauty of the garden but the beauty of our own life. We take ourselves for granted.

We know it. But we always hope for that day in the distant future when we can slow down and enjoy every minute of it.

That's a great idea, but you know what happens when we postpone something. They hardly get done. So what makes you think that this will be any different?

My only request is not to postpone this great experiment and discovery. Start it now. There is nothing for you to lose.

4

REACTION vs RESPONSE

Though the dictionary definitions for both these words are very similar there is scope to distinguish the two by saying 'Reaction' can be without much thought while 'Response' can be after considering the consequences. Of course, there are many stimuli that bring about immediate reactions and such reactions are needed to ensure safety and survival as a living being. But man being considered a superior creature is expected to act differently to certain stimuli.

Human civilization commenced from the day man sought to distinguish between reaction and response. Moral conduct is nothing but man's desire to respond to natural urges in ways that are acceptable to larger society. There are certain differences in the way various societies accept different behaviour, the important thing is that there are certain norms.

In this context it is interesting to note an ancient Hindu saying from Veda.

"Aahar nidra, bhaya maithhunam cha, samanametad pashurbhihsamana

dharmo hi tesanmadhiko vishesan dharmen pashubhihsamana"

(*Craving for food, sleep, intercourse are the same in both man and animal. Both man and animal are affected by fear. The only thing which differentiates man from animal, is the quantity of religion. Man is more religious. If a man lacks religiousness then he is more like an animal.)*

It appears man has come a long way in selecting acceptable behaviour when it comes to these gross and basic needs or stimuli. But it requires a higher level of discipline to manage behaviour when it comes to more subtle stimuli. If we are to group all the stimuli that we become subject to they can be broadly categorized in two groups – what **we like** and what we **do not like**. Throughout the day whether at work or at home constantly we face such stimuli. Some come as external manifestations by other persons or environment or circumstances. There are others that come within as feelings, motives and emotions.

The ability to respond to a situation considering the possible outcome is a skill. That is why some define the word *RESPONSIBILITY* as *RESPONSE-ABILITY.*

If it is an ability or a skill then one should be able to develop it by techniques and practice. Sometimes many acquire this ability over the years in life after objectively reflecting upon the past actions and consequences. Ability developed in that manner is called maturity. Yet the successful executive today cannot wait to be mature since he or she has to shoulder greater responsibilities very early in life. Then the question is how one can develop this skill?.

First the person should be able to notice what the stimulus is. Then consider the possible causes and the options available and choose the most suitable and act in the best possible manner. Though this sounds very obvious and logical on paper in real life it does not happen in ways we can see the different stages and the distinctions. In some instances it is only after seeing the consequences that we become aware of the previous steps. Therefore the crucial skill, is the ability to become aware of what happens now. It is really a very tricky task similar to balancing a mustard seed on the point of a pin.

Thoughts always come one after the other in sequence. Sometimes they happen so fast we do not see the sequencing at all, like improved memory chips being able to handle many millions of instructions per second.

When we start to drive, in the first few days it takes so much effort to coordinate different movements; – how to focus on the road while changing gears, handling the clutch and the brake etc, because they take place in quick succession. Once we master the skill they happen so fast we think they happen simultaneously.

If you recall how you started typing on the computer; first you search for letters one by one. You could then notice first the decision what word to type, then what letter to type first, after that the need to find where the corresponding key is and so on. But after mastering the keyboard it happens almost automatically. Yet the sequence is the same.

I gave these two examples to illustrate that the mind is capable of developing the skill to become aware of what goes on by learning to slow down first. This requires constantly observing mundane activities such as eating, drinking, brushing teeth, driving, ironing clothes, walking etc. What you need to do is to observe and become aware of what you are doing. The moment you start observing you will realize how the mind gets engaged in some other activity, thinking of something that happened in the past or that is to happen in the future. Come back to the activity in the present moment. If you continue this for some time, it is possible to develop the skill to notice what goes on in your mind pretty fast. Perhaps just before an action! The moment you become aware, you can think of what action to be taken and what consequence can be expected.

In order to develop the skill of becoming aware of what happens in the present moment we can use simple day-to-day activities as Practices. What you need to do is to carry out those tasks a bit slower so that you can observe the whole process. Remember these are only Practices to improve the skill. In the following pages a number of such activities are given. You can also discover your own Practice once you learn the art of practice.

We use the activity to bring the mind to the present moment.

5

WHY instead of WHAT

It was my third job. I was in my mid twenties. Having worked in that company for less than a year I had already decided to leave for another job. I discussed my intention with the General Manager of the company who was a well-respected elderly person. Although I communicated my intention to leave I had not handed in the letter of resignation but continued to work hard to finish all the assignments I had in hand. While I was doing this with a pure and professional attitude one day the GM made a remark to the effect that *"those who intend to leave can leave, we don't care"*.

I got very angry and hurt, came rushing to my desk, picked up the letter of resignation that was already typed and kept in my diary, with the intention of throwing it at him and walking out.

As I was pulling the letter from my diary a thought flashed across my mind.

"That's what he said. Now wait a minute, why did he say that?

"Why?" I thought for a while.

Around the same time that I had indicated my intention to resign, a few very senior employees of the company had left to start a rival business taking away some of the more profitable clients of the company. The loss of clients and staff and a long list of outstanding debtors from among the very clients who have left the company- were reason enough for a GM of a company to be in a state of stress and irritation. It is that frustration and tension that manifested as those unsavory words to me. That was 'WHY'.

I decided not to follow my anger, but to act as I originally planned, that is to continue my work until the month was over and leave the company having completed all the assignments I had in hand.

After leaving the company and joining a new place I realized within the first few months that it was not the place for me. I felt the previous place was better. I called the GM and asked whether I could come back. He said; "Of course, we never wanted to lose you, come back and start work."

Had I followed my instinct of anger, this conversation would never have been possible.

But later in life I realized that sudden flash of insight to look for the WHY instead of WHAT he did is a very important realization I had in life.

Of course sometimes our judgment about the WHY may be wrong, nevertheless it will open a new perspective of looking at things.

In nurturing relationships whether at work or otherwise trying to understand 'why' will always do more good.

Asking the 'why' forces us to consider the viewpoint of the other person. And in many instances such awareness of the other person's viewpoint will become the starting place for a solution. Not looking at that will only harden the position of either party.

This, however, does not mean that we give in to all that others do to us without asserting and taking appropriate responses, but it is suggested that this approach gives that mental space to choose the most appropriate Response which is not the habitual Reaction.

Even when facing seemingly positive dispositions of others, looking for WHY can help us understand underlying motives of the other party. In certain occasions asking the "why" would reveal completely different intentions than projected by the WHAT.

At an organizational level as well as at national level the more we try to understand the WHY of the other party our approach is much more strategic, harmonious, and mature. When we fail to do that our solutions are mostly short term. They can hardly lead to win-win solutions.

Creating this ability to stop and ask the question WHY is a mental capability that can be developed by learning to be mindful in other situations.

6

Choose a Practice that suits you

It is very easy to develop the skill of mindfulness by learning how to bring your mind to the present moment. You can do this by trying to come to the present moment by using the day-to-day activities of your life. In the next few pages there are twenty examples or practices to illustrate this point. When you go through them you will realize though the examples and practices are many the method is the same. You can of course choose the ones that suit you best. What I want to impress upon you is that you can use every moment you are awake to develop the skill of mindfulness.

You will discover that some are more effective than others. Let your own discoveries guide you to intensify practices suggested in this book as well as those you will discover.

Practice 1

Drink your morning cup of tea/coffee as if it is done for the first time in life
(What a silly idea you may think!)

Pour your tea into a ceramic cup with a handle. Keep it on a table and sit in front of it. Become aware of your sitting position – how you keep your feet and where you feel your body weight, the touch sensations on any part of the body, even the touch of your clothes on your body, the hard and soft sensations of your seat. It might be useful to slowly become aware of your whole body from tip to toe for a few seconds within your own mind.

Just be open to the sounds that surround you.

Do you hear the silence in between?

As you become aware of that silence look at the cup.

Become aware of any thoughts that come to your mind.

Sometimes the thoughts relating to expectations about the cup might come to your mind (such as likes, dislikes, memories about tea or any unrelated thoughts that may pop up), be aware and continue the observation, no need to analyze.

Observe the shape of the cup.

Look at the tea inside the cup.

Observe the colour, the golden ring right round the perimeter.

Now touch the cup and hold it and feel the warmth, the smoothness or the texture of its surface, the weight of the cup and bring it towards your mouth as slowly as possible.

Before you even bring your lips closer to the cup smell the aroma that emanates from the tea.

Does this aroma evoke any thoughts, memories, expectations? If so, become aware of them but don't analyze them. Notice and simply move on.

Observe the intention to drink.

Bring the cup closer to your mouth.

Become aware how your lips open up.

Observe the warm sensation on your lips.

Become aware of the process of tilting the cup and how hot tea touches your lips and tongue.

Take a sip to the mouth and take the cup away.

Observe the whole experience, what do you feel first – the wetness or the warmth?

The taste? What are the tastes that you notice and from which parts of the tongue or mouth do you get them?

Become aware of the process of swallowing the tea.

Hear the sound of swallowing.

Try to notice what happens to your breath at this moment. Are you inhaling, exhaling or holding the breath while swallowing?

Try to feel how the hot liquid flows through your throat.

Observe where you have the cup and once again become aware of your total being.

Repeat the whole process as many times as you can. The slower you do it the better it is to develop the ability to become aware of the present moment. You might notice suddenly that you are thinking of a totally unrelated subject instead of paying attention to drinking tea. Relax. come back to the present moment. Continue the experiment as long as you can.

Practice 2

Eating as a Practice to improve mindfulness

Eating is another routine activity that can be used to develop mindfulness. In many instances we spend a lot of time choosing particular types of food, scanning the menu at a restaurant and spending even more time shopping for our food items. But in reality do we really notice the taste of food, not in a gross sense but in the subtle fine form of taste? Do we remember what we had for dinner last night or lunch? Because it is a routine activity we engage in many other activities such as talking and reading while eating. The habit ensures that we continue to eat though there is parallel activity. Once we start to observe eating with mindfulness we will be able to appreciate how thoughts come one after the other.

To use eating as a Practice in mindfulness, start from the point of serving food to your plate. As you serve different types of food items observe the thoughts that come when you see them. Some you will like and some you will not like. Some you will want to try, some you will not want to try. Seeing some food items will evoke emotions, bring back even memories – just notice them.

Let me share an experience I had once in connection with eating.

"Once I got a Japanese set meal in a box while onboard a plane. In a corner there was an item which looked like caramel pudding – one of my favourite desserts. I thought I would eat it last. However there was an item which was sweet though. I eventually reached for my caramel pudding. As I brought the spoon closer to my mouth with the first scoop I was hopeful of experiencing the taste of caramel puddings I was used to. To my utter surprise it turned out to be a soya preparation with no sweet taste at all. Then I asked myself how much "old food" do we eat? In the sense how much we are preoccupied with the past tastes rather than experiencing the taste of what we eat right now!

If you eat using your fingers then you can focus on the touch sensation, if not focus on the process of mixing, cutting and bringing food to your mouth. Observe what happens to your mouth and like in the tea Practice observing the smell and the taste, watch the sound of munching and the feelings associated with swallowing.

This way we can come to the present moment.

Try listening to the body while eating. As food goes in be sensitive to the reduction of hunger that was there when you began eating. Actually, it makes a lot of sense to stop just before we feel really full.

Practice 3

Let us learn to walk

The secret of learning the skill of mindfulness is applying the technique to mundane activities that we do habitually and by slowing them down. If one were to count the number of blades of a rotating fan what is the best way? Stopping it, of course. Next best is to slow it down. It is the same principle that we use in this Practice.

Find a stretch of about ten to fifteen feet (3-4 Meters). This can be a part of your garden, a corridor in your home or the living apartment, or a stretch in a park or a beach.

If the weather permits be barefooted.

Stand still at one edge of the path. Have your hands on either side or in front or at the back. Observe the total being. How your feet feel the weight of your body, and the tensions of the muscles of your legs, back and even shoulders and arms. Keep observing the feelings and sensations of the whole body. You will be surprised at how many different sensations go on without our noticing.

Then make a decision to walk from your present position till the end of the path or the point you have identified in your own mind. Notice that until you decide to walk you don't move forward. Now begin walking very slowly. See whether you can break up the process of walking to its different stages. Such as lifting the foot, moving forward, bringing it down and touching the floor. While you take one foot forward and bring it down you will notice how the weight of the body moves towards the other foot. Keep focusing on the sensations coming from your sole. The touch sensation, the feeling of the weight, the bending, stretching, moving at every step.

While doing this too, you might find your mind drifting away to think of something else or a sound that reaches your ear can demand attention and so on. Here again relax and come back to walking. Slowly walk towards the end of the path. Once you reach the end stop and before stopping notice the intention to stop. When you come to a still position observe the sensations of the whole body from tip to toe.

Observe in your mind's eye your posture and the intention to turn back. Become aware of every single movement of the process of turning. Repeat the slow walk with total attention to the feet and the lower part of the body. Do this for about ten to fifteen minutes.

Once you figure out how to do this you can become mindful of walking even in other situations. Maybe your morning or evening walk on the beach, try becoming aware only of walking, how the wind touches your body, how the body moves, the rhythm of movement, the feeling in your feet, the sounds that you hear ... just notice and continue walking.

The objective of all these practices is to learn to bring the mind to the present moment and to the task at hand ... that is walking.

When doing this you will find many moments where you were engaged in other thoughts and even discussions with yourself.

Practice 4

Shower in the present moment

Often many of us get ideas and solutions to problems when we take a shower. The main reason being, it is a place where we are alone, and relatively free since we do not have to think much about what we have got to do since it is part of our habitual life. Unlike other faculties, the mind works best when it is quiet and undisturbed. Mindfulness developed as a skill helps us bring that stillness at will.

Let us see how we can practice mindfulness in the bathroom.

Take a simple routine like brushing teeth. Try and observe every step of the process – "being totally aware of the process of brushing teeth."

First, become aware of the intention to brush your teeth.

Then pick up the toothbrush, notice how you recognize your toothbrush from those of others. Feel the touch sensation, notice the intention to take toothpaste and pick up the tube, squeeze the toothpaste and become aware of the touch sensation and the intentions involved with the process.

You can also mentally label the activity as "taking" "squeezing" "closing the tube" "placing the tube back" and "brushing".

Listen to the sound of brushing and be aware of the whole process of brushing – the different movements of the brush, spitting etc. Become aware of the mental commands needed to make every movement. Yet we hardly notice those intentions or commands since it happens in such quick succession. If you stop brushing consciously you need to decide to do it again if the process is to continue. This observation will help you realize the process of intentions and actions.

As always, you will find your mind wandering away to things unrelated with brushing. Relax and come back to brushing your teeth.

When you shave you can try to do that also mindfully. You can count the number of times you pull the razor, the feeling and the sensations, and every step of the process. The trick is to bring the mind to the present moment to observe what happens, and the associated feelings, sensations and thoughts such as intentions.

If you do not have much time to do this experiment slowly (which is the normal reality) you can consider noticing the total activity with the thought that you are "Brushing, Brushing, or Shaving, Shaving" *Remember the objective of all these efforts is to develop the skill of bringing the mind to the present moment.*

While bathing you can either try to become aware of the whole process of bathing as one activity by labelling it mentally with a single word such as "Bathing, Bathing" or if time permits, break the activities to its small components. Become aware of the feeling as water touches the body, how you rub the body with your hands, the touch sensation, observe the intentions to change the movements of your hands, and the feelings when you use shampoo, soap or gel etc.

The art is in becoming one with bathing. Being totally aware of the whole process. Because it is such a habitual activity you will initially find it very difficult to observe the steps of bathing and to slow down the process. Then just try to remain only with bathing. Become aware at least of the predominant sensations.

Then take the process of drying yourself with the towel. Observe the intention. Which part of the body do you usually wipe first? Break the habit and become aware of the intention. Go on doing it but have your attention on the movements, sensations and any thoughts that arise.

When you do these kind of regular routine activities as your practices to develop the skill of being mindful, it is also important to become aware of the thoughts that come as a consequence of what we do. For instance, while washing yourself you might notice a scar or a lump or a pain that was not there and might have a series of other connected thoughts immediately. Just notice how this happens and say to yourself *THINKING, THINKING*!

Do not make trying to become mindful a serious affair. Treat it with a light heart. Make it a game you play with yourself. You have enough serious stuff to worry about. Practicing mindfulness shouldn't be one of them.

Practice 5

Get dressed mindfully

Another routine activity is getting dressed. First observe your habitual pattern of getting dressed. For instance, which leg do you use first when wearing the trousers or what hand do you first use when wearing a shirt or a jacket. These are opportunities to be more aware of the dressing process.

Observe touch sensations, movements of limbs and body and every single step of getting dressed. If you are a lady the process of doing makeup is a good moment to practice mindfulness.

Once you see yourself in the mirror observe what goes on in your mind. What you feel about yourself, about the dress etc. Here again the objective is to come to the present moment.

Practice 6

Driving mindfully is a pleasure

During the course of my life I have driven for over twenty years in Sri Lanka where traffic rules are observed as an exception! In a way, if you are not extra mindful you will never be able to complete the journey. That is the advantage of driving in places where traffic is chaotic. I have had three very small accidents involving another vehicle. On all three occasions – in fact, every time I had to apply the breaks suddenly – I realized that my mind was not on driving. I had been thinking of something else. I try to use my driving as a moment to develop the skill of being mindful.

If we use the process of driving as the main objective of our awareness and bring the mind back to driving every time the mind wanders into the past or future, then driving becomes your mind gym with no membership fees to be paid!

When you drive you do not focus your eyes on a particular spot or an object. You keep the whole view in your focus. This is the art of being aware of driving. If you focus on one you keep the others out. But in driving it is important to keep everything in view and focus only when it is required. For instance, when overtaking a vehicle we need to focus our attention to a specific area in our vision. This is a very good analogy that can be applied in the process of developing the skill of being mindful.

Traffic jams and traffic lights provide very good moments for us to improve our skill of mindfulness. See what happens to us when the traffic light turns red.

Observe the thoughts that arise and the reactions towards it. If you are in a hurry then your reaction is different to when you are not. In Sri Lanka sometimes vendors try to sell things at traffic lights. For them the red light turns to green very fast but to us who drive, it is very slow. This shows us there is no absolute measure except our mental disposition. You will learn to be mindful on your breath later in this book. Once you learn that, Red light can be a good moment to observe breath to come to the present moment.

Sometimes you come across careless drivers on the road. They really annoy you. Become aware of how you feel when confronted with such undesirable drivers. I have seen many scold them while being in the car with all the shutters up....

As you can see, driving is a very good practice to develop mindfulness.

Practice 7

A few minutes in the garden

You might have a garden or even a potted plant where you live. Or take a walk to the closest park. Try to observe the beauty of the garden and the trees. See what happens to your mind. It will begin its usual commentary. "The garden needs some care, that plant is dying, it needs fertilizer, I wish I had more time to spend on the garden, the garden of my next door neighbour is better" etc, etc.

When you become aware of the inner chatter come back to the present moment and just observe the garden as it is. Not how it should be or how it used to be. Both are not real. The reality is the garden as it is now. While being there observe how plants move in the wind, how butterflies and birds come. When you begin to observe the garden with mindfulness you will start to notice colours, shapes even the falling of a tiny flower petal can grab your attention.

Apply the same technique when observing the waves of the sea, a flowing water flow, a fountain, and even the sky with clouds. If you live in a place with less light pollution observe the sky in the night to notice the stars, the moon, and sunrise in the morning or the sunset in the evening

Be sensitive to the sounds of nature, the sounds of birds, sound of wind, just allow them to reach you and leave you. Notice that you can observe a sound only while it lasts, neither before it occurs nor after. This kind of observing nature to bring the mind to the present moment can be a truly significant experience.

Listen to the sounds that are near and those that come from afar. Try not to get involved with the sounds by analyzing them or trying to judge them as good or bad. Just allow them to reach you and leave you.

When you start observing sounds you will invariably observe the silence in between. Become aware of the silence as well. But note how the silence disappears the moment you verbalize that experience.

The mind finds it very difficult to be without this inner chatter. It is this habit that jumps in to label the silence to miss it as well.

> *Three kids promised each other to observe total silence for one hour. They lit a candle and sat around it with determination to observe silence. Within a few minutes a wind blew and the flame went out. The first kid said, "oh the candle went out" the second one responded, "hey we are not suppose to speak," and the third one announced, "see both of you spoke I am the only one who was silent."*
>
> *This is exactly what happens to us. Since we are not used to being in silence the moment there is silence we make a comment at least to say, "I am in silence now."*

Practice 8

Get close to nature

Gardening can be another interesting way to learn the art of becoming aware of what happens in the present moment. When you work in the garden, try to bring your mind to the activity that is at hand, instead of drifting into daydreams.

You can even try to synchronize your breath with the movement of your limbs as you work.

While you work you will have to be mindful of what needs to be done and many thoughts linked to that can be there. But be vigilant whether the mind drifts away to unrelated thoughts. That is natural. All that you will do is bring the mind to the point where you drifted away.

For instance, you might see a plant with a dead branch. You will then decide to cut it. While cutting the branch you can always think how to cut it, how to handle it etc, but if the mind goes to some past incidents linked to the plant, like where you bought it or who gave it, the day you planted it etc, then be aware you are in the past. Bring your mind gently to the present moment.

Practice 9

Ten Direction Look*

Try this and you will soon discover that you are on a different state of awareness.

Look straight into the horizon. From the level of the horizon lift your eyes just a wee bit, and stay there. In a little while you will begin to notice the whole area that surrounds you including the sky just above you, the place you are standing, and either sides of you. Maintain this look for a few seconds, you will even begin to feel the background behind you.

You will feel relaxed and attentive very soon.

*I learnt this during a short stay in a Zen-Christian hermitage in Japan. According to the master there (Rev Fr Oshida) this is a skill martial artists have to perfect. Accomplished martial artists stay in this mode so that they not only see the movements in the front and on either sides but become sensitive to any movements behind as well.

Practice 10

Cooking in the Present Moment

If you cook regularly then you can use it as well to improve the skill of being mindful. Actually, I know many who practice mindfulness in cooking and they say they enjoy it very much. Try to be with the process of cooking like you did with driving. You can engage in cooking without being aware and thinking about many other things but cooking. Instead, use cooking and all the steps related to cooking as a Practice to bring the mind to the present moment. You can certainly add a bit of love to your cooking as well!

Practice 11

Washing in the Present

Now you must be understanding how to use activities that are done as a routine to develop mindfulness or in other words, to bring the mind to the present moment.

Try practicing this while washing. At one level you can be aware of the washing process as a whole allowing the mind to guide you through the steps related to washing and wiping etc. If time permits try to observe the thoughts that keep coming while you wash. Some thoughts can be comments about the state of the object you wash and other thoughts can be related to the degree of cleanliness that emerges or about the steps that need to be taken while washing. This can be tried out when washing dishes or washing the car.

Practice 12

Music you listen to now

Some respond better to music. Play a piece of soothing music. Play any of the new age music softly and sit and relax. Allow the mind to be with the music without passing any judgment or involvement.

Pay attention only to the piece you hear NOW. Do not linger on the past melody nor anticipate continuation. Just be one with what goes on right now.

Practice 13

Breath our best friend

Sit in a quiet place with no disturbance or distractions. Sit with your back upright without leaning on the back of the chair. Gently close your eyes and bring your attention inwards. Observe all the feelings and sensations and become aware of the sitting posture. You can bring your mind's eye to the sole of your feet, observe the sensations there, slowly bring your mind along one leg up to your waist, and repeat the same with the other, observe the touch sensation of your thighs, the buttocks, how the muscles feel at the bottom and tension on the muscles of your back. Take your attention to the palms and see how they touch your thighs or each other, the heat and the touch sensations and slowly bring your attention along both arms one after the other up to the neck. Observe the feelings that are there along the neck and slowly try to observe all the other feelings that are there in your body. Any movements, tensions or any such feeling.

See whether you notice your breath. Try to observe where exactly you feel the process of breathing. Watch the rising and falling of your chest, and abdomen. Feel the touch sensation of the breath at the tip of your nostrils. Don't force your breath – let it be natural. If you really find it difficult to observe the feeling of breathing take a few deep breaths and see where the sensations are best felt.

Once you notice the inhaling and exhaling try to be with it observing the whole movement as if you are breathing for the first time.

If you find it difficult you may want to label the parts of the breath as "inhaling", "exhaling" but it is better if you can stop verbalizing as early as possible.

As you keep doing this for some time you might begin to observe the gap between the in breath and the out breath and when you do this you will feel your breath becoming finer and subtler. (Don't worry you are still breathing!)

When you do this for a few more minutes you might even feel a silence that was not experienced before, and become aware of that.

If you continue to sit for some more time you will begin to hear the sounds around you and might even notice different sensations in your body. Gently become aware of them and come back to the breath. Become aware of anything that may come to mind and return your attention to the breath.

Perhaps you will notice that you were thinking of something else instead of watching the breath. The moment you notice that, slowly come back to your breath. The mind is used to going all over like a child in a carnival, from one attraction to another. Don't force the mind to be still or be with the breath. Don't force. Then it behaves like a child. Instead allow the mind to be free but keep watching using the breath as your point of reference.

You can practice this for about twenty minutes every day and you will slowly pick up the art. No hurry – let it happen.

If you notice that many thoughts come in and the inner chatter that goes on nonstop, just starts watching without getting involved. Have a state of the mind that is similar to what you would observe when you are watching a magician perform wanting to see what happens next.

If you focus on your mind wanting to see the rising of thoughts after a few minutes you will realize that the new thoughts tend to shy away. The trick is not getting involved. When you feel that the inner chatter has subsided, slowly come back to the breath.

Keep doing this practice as long as you can. Better if you can do it regularly for a few minutes every day at the same time until it becomes a habit.

(There is a saying that if you want to inculcate a habit you need to practice it for at least 21 days.)

Breath is a natural activity that happens throughout the day until we die. Therefore, it is a very good base to develop mindfulness, since it is a constant object we can focus our attention on. We can neither watch the breath that has come and gone nor the breath to come – the next breath. Only the current breath can be observed. That too is constantly on the move.

Breath is available all the time and if you begin to notice you will observe breath changes according to our state of being. Well the easiest to observe is when we are excited. Then we tend to breathe fast. The breath is also short then. When we are relaxed we tend to breathe slowly and the breath is long.

By learning to observe our breath, we develop the skill of coming back to the present moment very fast. This is the main ability of mindfulness, being able to notice the present moment where everything happens.

For instance, at moments when you are agitated, angry, excited, or anxious, observe the breath for a few minutes. You can do this even during a meeting. The few breaths you observe will calm your mind bringing you back to the present moment. There is a space that is created through this awareness and in that state you will be able to see the situation with a more balanced and alert mind.

Through the practice you will begin to realize how the mind works and that thoughts come one after the other.

See the sequence:-

You get annoyed

You become aware that you are annoyed and now the thought you have is that of "knowing you are angry."

You observe your breath and now you have thoughts of becoming aware of the breath- not the thoughts of anger.

A few breaths later you are less agitated.

In that controlled state of mind you can respond to the situation rather than react.

Though this sounds so simple, it may not happen in the first instance. But it is like learning to drive. Once you are an experienced driver you can control the vehicle even at very high speeds in an emergency.

Let me share with you a personal experience of mine that happened about 30 years ago. I had just started to develop this skill of mindfulness. One day I got into a bus where I saw a man smoking. (At that time, the no smoking rule was not so strictly observed.) Being a young idealistic person I went up to him and asked him very politely not to smoke. He gave a sarcastic smile at me and continued to smoke. I knew I was getting annoyed and the next split second I pulled the cigarette out of his mouth and threw it out of the window. Then only did I realize the gravity of what I had done.

Once you are familiar with the art of observing the in-breath and the out-breath you can find many moments in the day amidst everything else to bring your mind back to it.

Next time when you are stuck in a traffic jam or at the red light, relax and observe the breath for a few minutes.

Try it out while waiting for a lift, waiting for a meeting to start, when the speech at the seminar is not relevant, before starting an important meeting, before joining an important telephone call, in between tasks while at your desk, or any time you want some peace of mind. All you need is to turn your mind inwards. The breath is there ready to help you come back to the present moment.

Take a glass of water into your hand. You will notice the movement of water. What is the best way to make water still? Leaving it on a surface for a few minutes"

Watching the breath is just like that. When you are stressed, tired and agitated watch the breath for a few seconds you will find calmness in your mind.

Practice 14

Travelling – moments to perfect the practice

Travelling provides us with many instances to practice mindfulness – specially a skill such as mindfulness in breath. When we use public transport or when we are driven by someone else we can use such times to practice. During long waits at airport lounges and hours we get to sit inside an airplane, when commuting in public transport such as train or bus we can use that time to close our eyes, turn our attention inwards and begin to observe our breath. In addition to improving mindfulness this method is a very good antidote for the anxiety and restlessness that is related with travel.

When planes get delayed, if you cannot make alternative arrangements there is no point in getting agitated. What are the practical steps that can be taken? Changing travel plans, informing the other end about the delay and making alternative arrangements. Do some work in the meantime. If any of these are not possible, thank the airline for giving you a moment to observe your breath! Learning to accept such situations in itself is a skill. Mindfulness helps us to accept the reality of a situation and do things that are practically possible, without wasting so much mental energy.

Travel also gives us an opportunity to be alone in solitude while being amidst a large crowd. Use that space to observe thoughts that come to your mind. Keep observing your own mind very attentively to see what thoughts do pop up.

Unless they are practically relevant at that moment learn to let go. Through these observations you will begin to notice your own intentions, the true intentions.

Practice 15

Practice in the shopping mall

Though this is the place where one least expects to practice mindfulness I found it to be a real testing ground to see how well one has mastered the skill of being mindful.

It is like taking the car to a highway after practicing on by-roads.

In a shopping mall, you are bombarded with various stimuli in the form of sounds, visuals, and even fragrances, tastes through sampling even if you just walk through. Try to observe your reactions and intentions that crop up when you are confronted with various stimuli. When being aware you will begin to see patterns in your thinking. Objects or types of people you like more than the others and what you really don't like. Later you can even review and ask yourself the question why you liked some objects more than the others. These are simple practices to get to know yourself better.

When you have to walk long stretches in a shopping mall why not try walking a distance mindfully being only with the walking. There is no need to really slow down.

Sit on a bench and try to observe all the sound that goes around without being involved. You will discover the usual silence in between the cacophony of the mall.

Practice 16

Art of relaxation

We tend to take our body for granted. We take more care of our cars than our physical body. We hardly let our body really relax. There is a simple routine we can follow to make our body relax. Do it at the end of a hard day's work. You will really feel refreshed.

Wear something light.

Lie flat on your back on a mat on the floor. Even the bed can be used provided it is a hard bed. Don't use pillows.

While lying become aware of your body top to toe.

Wriggle your body for a few seconds.

Let your hands lie alongside your body with palms open.

Gently close your eyes.

Imagine that you have a heavy weight tied to your legs. Raise one after the other a few inches from the floor and hold in that position for a count of ten and drop your leg and repeat for both legs.

Imagine you have to carry something very heavy and tighten your fists and raise your hands above the floor for a few inches and hold them like that for a count up to ten. Repeat for both hands.

Raise your head and try to see the toes and hold for a few seconds and let the head fall back gently.

Close your eyes and bring your attention to the tip of the right toe. Gently tell your mind "right toe relax" " right toe relax". Repeat this a for few times.

Right sole, upper sole relax, relax.

Ankle area, calf muscle …..keep commanding every single muscle of your right leg to relax. Repeat the commands until you feel the muscles are relaxed. If you feel tensions at any place, gently massage the place in your mind until it relaxes. Slowly bring the right leg consciousness to a point just below the navel. Repeat the same with the left leg and bring the left leg consciousness as well to the same spot.

Now take your attention to the right hand. From the fingertips to the shoulder, command every single muscle to relax. Visualize how each part of your hand gets relaxed and the weight being pulled to the ground.

Bring the right hand consciousness to a point at the centre of your chest. Repeat the same process to the left hand and bring the left hand consciousness to the same spot at the centre of the chest.

Take the mind to the place where leg consciousness was brought just below the navel and keep relaxing every single muscle from the navel area and upwards in circular motions.

Slowly bring the awareness of the trunk area to the center of the chest and continue moving up to the neck commanding every muscle to relax. Wherever you feel a tension gently massage the place in your thoughts. Be kind to your body and ask the muscles to relax, they will obey.

Now slowly bring your awareness along the neck relaxing the muscles of the neck, scan the back of your neck and come back to the front along the crown of your head relax the face muscles and bring the whole body consciousness to the point between the eyebrows and keep repeating the command telling the whole body to relax.

At this stage, try to keep your attention on your breath and be with the breath and breathe alone.

Sometimes you might even fall asleep for a few minutes. After five to ten minutes when you feel like it, slowly sit on the mat with your eyes still closed. If you can sit cross-legged then it is very easy – otherwise sit in a comfortable posture.

With your eyes closed, touch your whole body with both your palms as if you are washing your body. Bring both palms to cover your face gently and massage in a circular motion then rub both palms vigorously until they are warm. Cover both eyes with the warmed up palms for a few seconds and as you take the palms away from your eyes gently open your eyes.

Take a few deep breaths and slowly breathe out and gently stand up.

You are fresh again ... try doing this before you rush for your evening engagements.

You can practice this technique before you go to bed as well. You will fall asleep much faster than you can imagine.

Practice 17

Stretch

We can link our practicing of knowing what is going on even when we do our physical exercises. There are many practices that need fast physical movements, at the same time there are some movements that make us stretch our body very much and have to be done very slowly while synchronizing the breath as well.

Include such a practice regime in your routine in addition to your usual vigorous physical practices.

Do those slow moving practices trying to be totally aware of the movements, associated feelings, tensions, and the changes in the breath.

Practice 18

Close Windows before sleep

Sleep is one of the biggest gifts nature has given us. Yet many find it difficult to get sound sleep. When you fail to get a good sleep you are as tired as you were before going to bed. In deep sleep we do not even dream. All our faculties stop functioning.

One reason why we cannot get deep sleep is the various unfinished activities that go on in our mind. Worries of the past and anxiety about the future both cause the mind to keep working in such a way that we fail to get a good sleep.

There is a simple technique we can use before falling asleep to ensure that we get a deep sleep.

Once you are in bed, start recalling the whole day, either from the first thing in the morning till the time you go to bed, or from that moment till the beginning of the day. In this process you will notice what you did and tick off mentally without getting involved in that situation.

You will recall that you "woke up", "had bed tea", "got ready", "drove to office", "had a meeting with so and so" ...etc; not the details of what happened.

This is similar to closing the Windows session before you close down your computer. If it is not done properly then when you next start the computer there will be an error message saying that the "Windows was shut down incorrectly".

Our mind operates exactly in the same manner. If these subjects are allowed to linger without ticking them off they pop up during the sleep as dreams etc.

But when you tick off the tasks and incidents, they tend to get registered in the mind as 'closed' for the time being.

Actually if you are really tired you will not be able to complete the full day – half way through you might even fall asleep.

When you recall what you did, you will remember even the vehicles you noticed or overtook during the day or some people you met.

This is not an answer for all sleeping disorders. But certainly a simple method to ensure a good sleep.

Practice 19

Silence

One of the most difficult things for many of us is to keep quiet. Be without speaking. Or in today's context without communicating. Without uttering a word. We talk more now through our handheld devices.

I invite you to spend a day or a half-day without engaging in any external communications whether it is sending out information or receiving information. This would mean staying away from mobile phones, iPods, TVs, internet and even reading.

As I type these lines I can hear what goes on in your mind.

Believe me, if you do this and spend half a day or a full day by trying to bring your mind to the present moment, through engaging in the practices introduced so far you will find a completely different sense of relaxation. You will feel so calm inside you. As you stop engaging in communications slowly your inner chatter, too, will subside. This quietness will create so much inner space in your mind and you will feel stable and be in command of your being. If you can find time, try this for a couple of days at a stretch. You will begin to see things much clearer about yourself, about your relationships, fears, concerns, and your mind will provide you with brilliant solutions to the problems you may have.

Practice 20

Start slow to drive fast

Jumping out of the bed to start the day is very common, but we cannot do that (or we don't do it) with our cars. We slowly rev up the engine. We are in such a hurry when the computer takes its own cool time to boot up.

There is something to learn from this. I am not an expert on stress management but I have found that this jumping out of the bed business is an easy way to waste energy.

In nature things don't happen like that. Observe how a cat wakes up from its sleep. It first curls up and this is true for most animals. Even birds take a few seconds to take flight once, woken up from their sleep. There must be something that is needed to have this transition. At least the change of position from being horizontal to vertical must be having some impact on biological aspect of the body.

We definitely need to change the mode from sleeping to active which is like starting the computer from shut down position and not restarting from standby mode or hibernation mode. I bring this analogy because we behave in many ways like our computers. Life is not a hundred meter race but a marathon and we know how marathon runners approach the race.

I find starting the day slowly without rushing, helps build energy that can be sustained throughout most of the day.

Once awake, spending a few seconds reflecting on some good thoughts is very refreshing. Those with kids will find it satisfying to spend a few minutes with them. If not, spend a few minutes observing nature. In fact, now the urban areas have more birds than villages – listen to their songs and if you have a garden look at it, or you might have a plant growing on your balcony, see how it is growing. You do not need half an hour to do this, surely a few minutes can be spared for yourself.

Many drink water as they get up, which is supposed to be a very healthy habit. Most of us cannot start the day without our morning cup of tea. Try drinking the morning tea with total awareness about the whole process. You might have to wake up a few minutes early to start the day a bit slowly. And allow the things of the day take you on or you take them on as it comes. Rather than rushing early in the day and getting tired at the beginning of the day this approach is much more stable and steady. Try it and you will feel the difference.

7

Living Mindfully

All these practices help you develop the ability to bring your mind to the present moment and to become aware of what happens right now. Once you start practicing these and if you continue for some time this can be your way of being. As you can appreciate, this skill can be developed throughout the day and can be applied to any situation.

This needs to be continued for some time until you feel that it is your second nature. This is different to the usual habit of ours of not being aware of what really happens.

With this you learn to observe your own thoughts as they arise. This is a very important skill. We tend to ignore our own feelings, likes, dislikes, prejudices when we do things. How we act is directly influenced by how we think. The more you become aware of your own intentions and motives you will be more sensitive to your own being. You can become your own coach, so to say. Or when you need to get guidance you will know precisely where you need help. You will learn from every interaction in life being able to observe things as objectively as possible. The chapters ahead in this booklet illustrate many such applications.

You will, in short, begin to read the book that is closest to you – that is your life.

With this increased awareness of your own thoughts you begin to see clearly how you react to external stimuli and it paves the way to a new state of being.

Living with awareness is like applying a new operating system that improves the performance of your computer. The mindfulness based awareness helps you see things clearer and you will be able to go beyond the obvious paradigms and tap in to a deeper potential that was inhibited otherwise.

Through experience we know how answers to many problems flash through our mind when we take a shower. Because it is a state where the mind is free without being disturbed by constant chatter. By learning to become aware you master the art of reaching that state of calmness at your will. Then your mind operates at its peak performance.

Once you start developing mindfulness as a skill it can be a part of your life. It will be the way you operate, it is going to be your playing field. As a result of this you will have a greater sensitivity to your own thoughts, emotions and feelings. How you respond to the world and how you relate to the world will be guided by this awareness state. You will be able to keep your cool, you will feel that you are in control of a situation rather than you being dictated by the situation.

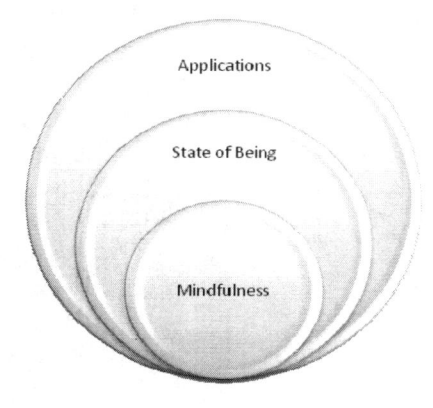

Becoming aware helps you influence how you relate to yourself as well as how you relate to others and to situations. In this state you become more and more congruent with your own intentions and actions. Your state of being begins to be one of freedom. Your attitude towards yourself as well as to the external world will be guided by this new state of being.

You will discover that the journey is as enjoyable as much as the destination. Instead of waiting to become happy at a distant date you will be happy now. You will be able to bring harmony into your life by becoming aware, bringing in all aspects of your life to a cohesive whole. You will be able to link your day-to-day activity to a higher purpose than pure activities that drive you to achieve mundane goals. You will be able to discover deeper meaning in your life by way of becoming constantly aware of your being.

As you improve your mindfulness you will be able to see clearer your own thoughts as mentioned already. This ability helps you gain insights as to how things happen in life. Once realized they become your first hand insights not like the knowledge that is gained by reading a book or the intellectual understanding that comes by way of reflection.

In your geography lesson you learn the temperature of different countries. That is knowledge.

Depending on where you live you can compare your local temperature with that of another country and have an intellectual understanding as to what it would be to live in a country with that temperature e.g. sub zero or desert.

If you arrive in that country and experience that temperature you realize it firsthand. There is no need for any intellectual understanding at that stage. It is your first hand experience.

Insights gained through mindfulness are like that.

Reflections:-

Out of those twenty practices which was the one you found most useful and practical?

What are the new practices you discovered in your life?

In this moment

8

Name it to Miss it

According to a popular Zen story, the teacher and his student went on an evening walk. The walk took them to the top of a mountain and from there they could see the sun set in the distant horizon. It was so beautiful the student commented, "Wow what a beautiful sunset," The master did not say anything until they returned to the centre. He called the student and said, "From tomorrow you need not come to observe, sunset with me." The student was surprised and asked him why? "You did not observe the sunset. You only commented. I would rather go with a person who will enjoy the sunset." The student was really puzzled, he thought that he had really enjoyed the sunset. But the master later told him, the moment he had said "it is a beautiful sunset" he had stopped observing and experiencing the sunset.

We are so used to playing commentator throughout the day. Even when we see a beautiful sunset or something beautiful we immediately comment, "Wow, I wish I had my camera," or nudge the bystander to observe the beauty of the object. So what is wrong with that? There is nothing wrong with it except that this habitual reaction stops us from really seeing it.

It is only during this uninterrupted moment of observation that the realization happens. Remember the story of Archimedes, who discovered the answer to the question when he got into the bathtub; how it occurred to Newton that gravitation pulls things to earth when sitting under an apple tree in a pensive mood. Even to us answers to many questions come when we least expect it, sometimes while taking a shower, or in a pensive mood when we are not thinking about it, when the mind is silent for a moment. Even as students we came across many moments when we just realized the method to solve a maths problem and thought "*aha!*"

For insights to come, the mind needs to be quiet, **The deeper the silence the sharper the clarity.** The biggest disturbance to this much required quietness is the constant inner chatter and our habit of wanting to name and give a commentary to what we observe.

The moment we give a name to it the observation stops. The moment a label is put on, it has to go to the appropriate place in the mind and most of the time that itself stops further investigation. This is the habitual nature of the mind. We bring this habit very much to the workplace as well.

For instance, you show a team of employees a video clip of a well-functioning work situation or a top performing sports team and ask them what they saw. The answers will be phrases like "team work", "commitment" or "communication". Are they real observations or are they labels? Or a name given to a certain phenomenon. Such a statement really does not help us learn from a situation. Without observing the specific things that happen one cannot learn or repeat the same action. It is like watching a dance. Most people will say it is a beautiful dance. But those who are very observant of the details of the movement who go beyond the exclamation *'it is a beautiful dance'* only will be able to learn the steps and repeat the same performance or improve on it.

Naming is such a powerful habit that stops investigation. I think it is the mind's need to reach a state of equilibrium that demands a name. That is the normal state. You encounter something, there is a need to know what it is, give it a name and the cycle is complete. Even at a gross level we need to go beyond the naming if we are to really observe what happens. Innovations, improvements come only when such observations occur. That is why when we see a new product that solves such obvious problems we immediately grab it.

Developing this ability to observe without stopping by giving a name to it can be considered important even in the world of commerce. By learning to keep the mind quiet and becoming aware of the naming process we can develop this capability.

9

The biggest noise

Once I was observing a *pooja* (a religious offering) at the home of one of my Hindu friends in India. I love listening to those sacred chantings. To my surprise the priest who conducted the *pooja* at my friend's place did not chant them aloud. I asked my friend why? He posed a question before answering me.

"If you ring a bell in a large open field, or in a closed room, where will you hear the sound strongest? He himself answered: "The loudest sound comes when they are chanted inside the heart."

***** ***** ******

The other day I was at a public meeting, where there was a mixed audience including a group of small children who did not know the importance or the significance of the event. Just before the invited speaker started his speech the kids started to talk to each other. Then one of the adults asked them to be silent.

****

These two unrelated incidents made me wonder from where we get disturbed most when we listen. Is it from the external noises or from the internal noises ?.

External noises do pose many challenges like the sound of another person's voice. But the biggest barrier I think, comes mostly from the inner chatter that goes on without any interruption. When the audience is in absolute silence, when the acoustics are perfect, when the speaker does a good job there are yet many moments where we drift away to endless discussions of inner chatter.

When observed carefully most of this inner chattering is linked to the past and to the future. It leads us to incidents that happened in the past and we re-live the whole situation. We engage in discussions with the very people, with whom we had those discussions, and new ideas come as to what we could have spoken etc, etc. Or we re-live those moments in the past experiencing all the emotions that were attached to them. Mind you, all this occurs while the speaker is still talking.

The future is no different. We write our own screenplay and take part in the show. Some of these scripts have much more adventure than the biggest thrillers!

Some of this inner chatter take the form of a commentator that gives very subjective views telling us positive as well as negative possibilities. Sometimes they take the form of conversations, while on other occasions they take the form of pictures and even the form of feelings, as if they are real.

If this is the way we act most of the time, isn't it amazing how we can get about our daily activities without more disasters. Well – the answer is that we mostly shift between spurs of attention and inattention.

Whenever I have to apply brakes suddenly while driving, I think in that split second my attention was not on driving but was on something else.

At the same time when we are really engrossed with some activity we do not hear any other sounds either. This shows the power of attention. So we can assume how we move from attention to inattention from moment to moment.

The ability to bring the mind back to the present moment to pay attention to the activity that is in hand can be considered a skill that can be developed. But this cannot be done by forcing the mind to come to the present moment. It is like asking kids to be silent. They are silent when they are engrossed in their own activities.

If we allow the mind to be still for some time, without getting engaged in this constant chatter we will experience brief moments of silence. In this silence we can realize that even the concept of present is transient.

Such clarity helps us to focus on issues with a high degree of freedom so that we can hear the other person's point of view better, to see more possibilities as to how a problem can be solved without holding on to past views and memories, focusing and discovering new opportunities and possibilities whether they are in the world of business or in the world of day-to-day living.

10

The finger and the moon

During our childhood we believed that if we pointed our fingers at the rainbow it would disappear.

I really do not know whether today's kids subscribe to such ideas. What I want to discuss is not the possible effect of pointing at the rainbow but the role of the finger when pointing to something.

When we use the finger to focus attention of the others towards an object in the distance the finger acts as a pointer. The observation of the object is the responsibility of the other person. In this activity we never identify the finger with the object it is pointed at. But in many other situations we tend to follow something different. For instance, the WORD.

Words are a collection of sounds when spoken, and collection of letters or truly a collection of symbols when in the written or printed form. In summary, the word is also a symbol as much as a symbol, too, can elicit many words. For instance, a traffic sign evokes not only a set of words but many associations as well. This series of thoughts can include, what the sign means, consequences if not followed, past experiences if any, the impact the observation of the rule will have on the current journey, similar signs and rules in other countries, the traffic conditions in the country, reactions to that and so on.

Doesn't the same hold true for words? To understand a word, first the meaning of that word should be stored in our memory. Unlike a dictionary meaning, the memory associates many links to a word other than the direct meaning to it. In most instances this is subjective to the history of the person such as the personal experiences associated with the word, his/her formal and informal education, and the socio cultural background that is associated with the word. All these come to play when we hear or read a word.

While in technical fields and subjects there are accepted definitions to words, in most other areas that affect human beliefs and relationships this is not so although there are acceptable meanings. Even in technical fields meanings of certain statements have got different definitions as a result of changes across time or sometimes owing to legal interpretations.

Take a simple word like 'pain'. If a person were to say "I am in pain", we think and even say that we understand what he means. But can we really feel what the pain is? During certain medical treatment processes the doctors and nurses ask patients to describe the degree of the pain using a scale of one to ten. But this is so subjective from person to person since different people have different pain thresholds. If a close friend or a member of the family who is very close says that he or she is in severe pain that will elicit a different understanding and feeling. If the relationship is so close you might even feel the pain of the other person but it will not be so for a distant third person. This is true for many of the words we use to communicate.

Actually the word can only point us towards the direction of understanding. but the actual understanding is a very personal experience. Words can take us to the point of understanding and realization and at that point of understanding, the word ceases to be of any relevance. The spontaneous expressions that come at moments of realization are monosyllable sounds rather than words. Hence expressions such as '*aha*' Even a universal feeling such as LOVE is not the word love. Take examples closer to you and you will realize how difficult it is to explain exactly how we feel, using words. The word is only an approximation to the real thing that is being described by the word. Yet words have their use similar to the finger that helps us focus our attention on an object that is in a distant location. Words may help us realize something, but the realization takes place at the end of the word.

In the world, however, there are so many conflicts because of the words and their interpretations by those who mistake the word to be the ultimate truth. Unless we realize that the word is not the actual experience, or the object that is being referred to, we can get so preoccupied with it and can even go to war for the sake of it

Accepting this limitation of word, **that the description is not the described** gives us greater freedom to use it.

11

Can we really listen?

"To help we need to understand, to understand we need to listen, to listen we need to be quiet"

It is worth exploring whether we can really listen – listen quietly.

Listening is active hearing. Understanding means in the normal sense giving the same meaning to a set of sounds that the other person is intending. *I assume that you give the same meaning I intend when you read the words I write.* At the level of the language even this is sometimes difficult. There are many words that give different meanings when said in different languages. In the world of business there are many stories how certain brands have failed in different countries simply because the word sounds negative in such markets. There are many more examples that prove the sounds of the language we call words do not have unique meanings. In different contexts the same word can mean different things. 'Sentence' in grammar is different in meaning when one is given the "death sentence".

As we listen to the sounds or words of the other person we listen to them with all our past history. In fact, if not it were for the past we would not understand them at all. The moment we say we 'understand', it means that we have heard that sound before and know what it connotes. But this past knowledge and conditioning itself can bring in so much limitation to our ability to listen. In reality it is nearly impossible to listen without this past conditioning. Our past experiences, learning, prejudices – all these condition how we perceive a particular sound or a word. Childhood experiences, social background, life experiences, professional specialty – all these play a very important role in conditioning as to how we understand the present experience, and how we judge it.

The moment we hear a sound, the brain, our computer recognizes it as a sound, looks for similar sounds recorded in the past and compares the present sound with past associations and helps us to recognize it for what it is. Immediately after this recognition, we form a certain judgment or an opinion about it based on the past. This leads to measuring it, or classifying it, agreeing or disagreeing with it, liking or disliking it, and a whole series of emotions emerge, as a result of this judgment. This process then generates a whole heap of actions and reactions within the mind and it begins the inner chatter as a consequence. But while this is going through in our mind the other person may be continuing to speak. Because we are involved in this inner chatter we hardly hear the other person's words.

If the other person's word triggers a powerful emotion or a memory then our mind will get entangled with that memory or the emotion and there will be a proliferation of related thoughts and emotions. Instead of listening, we will then search for answers, responses and arguments to either agree or disagree with the statement of the other person. This we see very clearly when people argue. In the height of arguments neither party answers to the other person.

Hence the ability to listen without being judgmental, without engaging in the inner chatter, really silently at least to the extent of not engaging in the process of counter arguments can be considered a very high skill. It is a skill that can be cultivated by learning to be aware of what happens within the mind. Telling the mind to listen without being judgmental, conditioning the mind to listen with the intention of understanding not only the word but the meaning, we can develop this art of non-interfering listening. Contrary to common belief and our habit such listening help resolves issues much faster than the habitual way of listening with inner chatter. When we listen in this way the other person feels that and it builds trust and confidence because in this process you give total attention to what is being said.

When we become aware of the process of internal interpretations and limitations then we know that our reactions are influenced to that degree. This takes us to the sphere of responding rather than habitual reaction.

12

Listening is speaking

Once a manager was walking past a large department. A girl with swollen eyes caught his attention. He casually asked her what was wrong with her. She said nothing but gave him a blank look. She rose from her seat and asked, "Boss can I speak with you?" He said "yes" and asked the girl to come to his office.

She walked into his office, sat and slowly started to relate a story – the story of her life. She explained what a painful life she had had as a child and how she had got a meaning to life when she found her longstanding boyfriend. For almost three years she cooked and brought him lunch since he lived close to her home and on weekends she offered to wash his clothes. They were to get engaged, dresses and rings were made and her manager was invited to be the attesting witness. Just two days before, she was told that he could not get his parents' permission and they could not get engaged. Hearing this shocking news, her mother, who had been a widow for over 10 years had a heart attack. While she related the whole story the manager merely listened. He knew she was a good worker. He was really concerned. What the girl wanted at that moment was someone who would listen to her story without judging her, without interrupting her for it was too much for her to carry. Later she had told him that his patient listening prevented her from taking her life.

***

A factory was reporting a sharp drop in productivity. The head of finance decided to spend a few days in this factory located out of the city, to see what exactly was happening. The workforce was predominantly female. She got them to stop work an hour early one day and having provided them with papers and colours asked them to draw anything they would like. She wanted everyone to draw something irrespective of whether they could draw or not. The result was amazing. Most of the drawings had violence as the theme. She started speaking with a few girls at random. What she learnt was shocking. Most of the girls had been abused by the factory manager in exchange for providing a job.

The head of finance immediately got the factory manager out, and a few other changes to improve the living conditions. In a few months the productivity improved.

***

According to a Zen story a king has asked his sons to listen to the sounds of a forest as a way to train them. They went deeper into the jungle where the silence was intense and yet they were able to hear very subtle sounds. The father's advice was to "listen to the sound of pinewoods when there was no blowing".

A child had asked two teachers in school on a Friday whether he could speak with either of them but they were too busy and suggested that the child come to meet one of them on Monday. Over the weekend the child committed suicide.

***

Once, a factory manager attended the funeral of a lathe machine operator in his factory. The widow showed him a large collection of short stories written by her late husband which were never published. The manger asked himself who was dead – the machine operator or the writer?

***

I shared all these stories to focus on the need to listen to our fellow human beings who may be your co-workers. In this over-populated world individuals are very lonely. Many come from homes where there is hardly any listening. We tend to think conversations are about talking. But the more important part of conversation is listening, listening without judging and interfering with our own views and prejudices. For many problems the solutions are found by those who are facing the problem themselves but allowing them to share the problem with you and gently asking them to look at the options can make a world of difference to that person.

If you master the art of becoming aware of what happens with you, the same sensitivity will improve the ability to be more sensitive to your colleague. You will discover many life changing, self-satisfying moments by being open to the lives of others around you.

13

Don't waste the arrow

One day I was observing a beautiful mountain peak. There was nothing between me and the peak. A cloud came and I lost the peak. Later as I was again watching it, I realized that I had been thinking of many things and I had not seen the peak for a long time.

The moral of the experience to me was that, more than external distractions, our own thoughts can distract us from the goal. This is something to do with focus.

A Zen master was to conduct a test for his three best students. The test was to shoot the target, which was the eye of a painted bird placed on a branch of a tree, with an arrow. The first student came and started focusing on the target. The master asked what he could see. "I can see the bird on the branch," he said.

"Don't waste the arrow," said the master.

Next was the second student. He, too, focused for a long time and just before he was to release the arrow from the bow the master asked the same question. "I can see the bird," was his reply, too.

"Don't waste the arrow," was the master's response again.

Then it was the chance of the third student.

His answer to the question after a much longer period was "I can see the EYE."

The master said, "Go ahead."

This illustrates the power of focus.

In our life whether in work or otherwise it does not take a lot to lose focus. We set very lofty goals in the beginning and agree on strategies. But in implementing we forget both the target and the strategy – sometimes due to real external challenges and changes. But in more instances than not, such changes happen owing to simple distractions that take our focus away. When we are about to embark on a strategy one important stake holder would pose a question or a comment and this would make us lose focus. This is not to say that we should not take views from others but I think the issue is at what point do we do this?

Compared to people like the Japanese who take a long time to agree on the goal and the strategy, there are many others who agree on these very quickly and at the same time change their goals also very quickly. So we tend to correct as we go along and sometimes the corrections take us back to where we start or even to a situation worse than that.

I am sure you will be able to spot many examples at organizational level as well as national and at individual level.

It is true that in many a journey's path corrections are a must. Any airline pilot will vouch for this. During the flight path they make many corrections in response to the environmental changes, but they do not lose focus of the target and the strategy.

Maintaining focus can be a skill that can be developed by learning to be constantly observing how the mind works, how the mind moves away from what is at hand. It is at this individual level that the ability to be focused should be developed.

Reflections:-

Did you try to observe your mind in the same way?

What are the discoveries you made for yourself?

Built around me

14

Dreaming, Day dreaming and Thinking

There must be a reason why there are three words to describe these mental activities. Dreaming happens only when we sleep. According to scientists "a **dream** is a succession of images, sounds or emotions which the mind experiences during sleep."(Wikipedia) But when we dream they are so real. We see, hear, feel, smell, taste, experience, do just as when we are awake. One may call it virtual reality in a way. We seem to have very little control over what we get in our dreams except very often most of our dreams have links to the activities and things we do during the day or prior to sleep.

Daydreaming takes place while we are supposed to be awake. It can be positive as well as negative. A person who buys a sweep ticket can win the lottery, become rich and do many things in a few seconds of daydreaming. Similarly, a person who is bitten by a mosquito can contract dengu, get sick, become very weak, enter hospital, spend many days, with the loved ones coming to see him in hospital. Because of hospitalization he could lose a major opportunity in business or in life, and it can cause considerable damage to his entire future plans either personally or for the organization. But the mosquito can be an innocent harmless one!

But then what is it that we call THINKING? Thinking can be reflecting in our mind a situation or an issue considering various possibilities, options, outcomes, consequences etc. But unless we are aware, the process of thinking can also drift away into daydreaming. While daydreaming is hardly productive, and in most instances it is counterproductive, thinking can be useful and productive.

If we take a close look at how we spend time from a mental perspective, we tend to move either into the past or to the future unless gainfully engaged in some activity. Even while engaged in a very serious activity our mind can quickly pick up something from the past, or can prompt us to pay attention to a situation in the future. Most of our worries, if not all our worries, are linked to our past. There is very little we can do about those. Some are mistakes we have made that cannot be undone, and our anxieties and stresses come from the future, like the anxiety about going to the dentist. You dread the moment and think of the pain and the discomfort long before reaching the doctor. If the doctor says that no filling is needed, all that anxiety or tension entertained was of no use. While we tend to show capability in thinking rationally, when it comes to certain professional issues when no people are involved, this ability to be logical becomes less when either ourselves or others are involved in the situation.

If we can create a distinction between passive thinking and active thinking we can handle most situations. Passive thinking is more like daydreaming. We allow the story to unfold on its own. This is like an unedited story with many visuals but without a proper link. In most instances when we say we are thinking of something, the generation of thoughts take the form of a daydream and it becomes one of confusion rather than clarity. It ends up building tension and anxiety. Whereas if the problem is identified and if it is approached in a manner that is structured and logical that will bring us closer to a proper solution. In fact, when people are counselled one thing the counsellors do is to help the person to approach the question with a balanced mind to see different options.

Many find it useful to write the problem on a piece of paper and work on it writing or drawing rather than pure thinking. However, the best solution comes when the thinking, even logically, is stopped. The process of analyzing, looking at the issue and all such deliberations will help in reaching a solution.

Different people have different ways and rhythms of realizing. The important thing is identifying the method most suited for the individual.

However, the critical thing is being able to be aware to realize when one is not thinking but daydreaming. This is a skill that can be developed by practice.

15

Being alone and feeling lonely

Lonely- *solitary, companionless, isolated, sad because without friends or companions.*
Alone- *not with others, oneself without assistance*

There are many moments we feel lonely, even when we are among large crowds. A feeling sometimes we are scared of. The response to this feeling takes many forms and manifests itself in different ways of reactions and behaviours. Most of the time we respond to this feeling by trying to escape from it. We do not like to accept it, hence the reactions and responses we do not see as escaping from loneliness. We seek external opportunities to fill this emptiness.

Many of our socializing needs stem from this scary feeling of loneliness. When feeling lonely we do so many things. The latest habit is turning on the mobile phone or the blackberry for e-mails, SMS, calls. Means such as "Facebook" and "twitter" all thrive on this need to get away from the feeling of loneliness. Technology also provides many interesting ways of escape from this feeling while being physically where you are. 'iPod' allows you to listen to the music you love, retail therapy, and going out all help us to escape from this scary feeling of loneliness.

In another dimension, in our working life we also experience many moments of being lonely. When, for instance, you are the only person who sees a particular point of view, or believes in a particular solution to a problem, when others do not share your idea and belief. The feeling of loneliness can happen even in a tense meeting. The reactions to such feeling can vary from total withdrawal to aggression. Instead of trying to find ways and means either to see the other person's point of view to re examine your own view or to find ways and means to present your idea in a way that can be palatable or acceptable to the others. This is a skill that needs to be developed and a mental state that needs to be recognized.

In order to recognize and to become aware of this state of mind it is important that we develop the ability to observe and be sensitive to what goes, in our mind as it is. In many instances our own minds play tricks on us without letting us realize what really goes on. When one is lonely the mind makes many suggestions that drive us to behaviours that we justify rather than accepting that we feel lonely.

In developing this skill it is important to learn to be alone. To be alone is a conscious decision. It is a choice we can make not a consequence. We need time and space to be alone. When we choose to be alone we have the freedom to observe our own thoughts, to listen to our own voice, which when allowed to echo tells things without those protective labels. When you decide to take a walk without listening to your "i Pod" and recorded music you can experience this power of being alone. Since you choose to be alone you will not have to feel lonely. Being alone for short spells is very important for the mind to find its own space, the rhythm and patterns. Learning to be alone is an art and it needs some courage for we are so used to being with the crowd either physically or psychologically.

Learning to be alone and doing it very frequently improves the ability to be sensitive to what goes within and what goes around. This is a very important survival skill even in the corporate jungle – a primitive capability we would have had before all this sophistication became part of our overall conditioning.

16

To be alone is a skill

There is so much emphasis on the development of skills pertaining to being with a crowd. How to meet people, how to introduce oneself, how to take on cultural sensitivities and nuances, how to make effective presentations, social etiquette – the list is endless. There is no argument that the need to be effective in a crowd and in the larger society is absolutely necessary. But there is another skill that is even more critical to develop, that is, to be alone.

From childhood we are trained and conditioned to be among a crowd physically. But even in a large crowd one can feel really lonely either because of the lack of any known persons, or because of another social barrier such as language, or a personal circumstance that keeps the person totally preoccupied with thoughts pertaining to a particular thing. The person who has to make a presentation in front of a large or hostile audience can feel lonely. A sportsman also can have the same feeling of loneliness in front of thousands of spectators. Sometimes these can be very painful for a person to experience. For instance, being away from home and loved ones can cause unbearable loneliness. It must be this reason why wrong-doers are confined to solitary cells as prisoners. It has been in use to punish people from time immemorial. In the teachings of the Buddha the biggest punishment is called *"brahma danda"*: that is to avoid speaking with a person.

Even if we are not punished, there can be many moments in life, when we will have to experience loneliness. Sometimes owing to physical ailments, sometimes, owing to other circumstances when it is not possible to communicate with others specially loved ones and those who share similar thoughts, we feel loneliness. There are also moments when we have to associate with people who do not share our ideas, people we do not like. At the same time when we miss the association with those whom we like we feel lonely. On many occasions it is a feeling that is harder to bear than physical pain.

The painful experience of being lonely can make a person vulnerable to many other influences.

When observed closely, loneliness can be seen as a state of mind when there isn't another person with whom one can share life whether it is in terms of physical contact or emotional contact. When explored deeply it can be seen that the main reason for this feeling of loneliness arises from life's longing nature to become, to continue and the lack or inability to control the phenomenon that is life.

That is why, when feeling lonely we feel insecure. Familiarity gives a sense of security. For instance, old parents prefer to be at their traditional homes even by themselves rather than in unfamiliar urban houses of their children. This is the sense of security and comfort that comes from familiarity.

In working life we get the same sense of security when we have to deal with subjects that are familiar to us, things that we have been doing in the past, and the things that are from our fields of professional upbringing.

When individuals reach higher positions in organizations they are expected to perform a different set of functions than in their previous positions. This can mean being in unfamiliar territory. In many instances the persons at the top have to make final decisions carrying the responsibility and accountability of the consequences alone. In some other situations the person at the top is expected to make decisions that are not popular. On another occasion, the person will have to defend a view that is completely different from the others. Instead of the larger group of people with whom he or she had to work in the past, once at the top he may have to work with a few others at the same level who may, very often be more interested in their own area of work causing the person to feel lonely.

This loneliness causes the person to feel insecure. This feeling can be very stressful and make the person vulnerable. In response the person can find ways to micromanage work making subordinates feel they are being interfered with or he will want to engage many others for unnecessary discussions. It is this very feeling of loneliness that opens the persons at the top to be easy targets of those who thrive by carrying tales. They become informants and thrive on that power base placing the new man at the top at great risk.

Some others resort to various other stimulants such as drugs, alcohol, even sex to fill this emptiness.

In this context it can be seen how important it is to develop the skill of being alone, by constantly choosing to do so. It requires bigger inner strength and more training than the social skills that are empirically taught.

17

The Paradigm of "I"

Paradigm shift (or **revolutionary science**) is the term used by Thomas Kuhn in his influential book *The Structure of Scientific Revolutions* (1962) to describe a change in the basic assumptions, or paradigms, within the ruling theory of science.

But in the world of commerce we use the phrase paradigm and paradigm shifts very freely now to relate to particular thinking patterns and the limitations brought about by those and moments moving out of those patterns.

It is said that when a Swiss engineer invented the quartz watch the industry who were the pioneers of the watch industry in the world, did not accept it as a viable option. However companies like SEIKO adopted it and today the watch is not just a chronometer but a fashion item, a utility item that anyone can buy.

Until Copernicus challenged it, the view was that the earth is the centre of the universe. He challenged the established paradigm or the frame of reference at that time.

As humans we need a certain framework to relate to the world. Yet this framework itself can limit our ability to perceive the world.

In many instances technological innovations challenge the existing paradigms and replace them with new paradigms. Until the introduction of the mobile phone, the telephone was a piece of fixed equipment – a symbol of importance and authority. Today the telephone is at hand whenever you want to communicate with someone. The users also want the equipment to facilitate not only audio communications but visual communications as well.

Most of these paradigms or conditionings of our thoughts are due to various external factors such as our upbringing, education, experience, media and other influences. Some of this manifests as professional, political, ethnic limitations or as views.

Yet the most subtle is the paradigm of "I".

Let us explore this. If someone were to comment on what you have done by saying, "You have done a GOOD JOB," how would you feel? You feel good. But what was the message?. It was the job you did that was good; not you the person. But that is how we feel. We equate ourselves to what we do, what we think, and what we experience. There is nothing good or bad about it. It is the way it is. The implication, however, is that this perception helps us to form our self image. All of us have a certain image about ourselves and we are pretty possessive about it. Just to illustrate the point. Will you give a randomly picked photo of yourself to be published in a newsletter or will you look for the one where you look good? It is the picture where you look best that you will release because the picture in that photo is the image you have about yourself. **It is our conditioning**.

The implication of this process, is that we identify ourselves with the ideas we express as 'I' and 'mine'. So at a meeting when my idea is challenged by someone who sees some obvious flaws in it, I read it as that person criticizing me without me realizing that the moment an idea is expressed it is in the public domain and is subject to public scrutiny. What is my reaction? I can be very upset and embarrassed, or, be very arrogant and even violent. When that person comes up with an idea next time round, my reaction would be to object even without reason just because he criticized me! (Of course he had only criticized my idea). This is how the paradigm of 'I' prevents us from proper communication or a constructive dialogue.

This does not mean that one should not protect or stand by his or her own ideas and work. It must certainly be done but one should be aware of the operating model. Once you realize it, you are free to see things without being coloured by personal prejudice. This is the beginning of a true dialogue which is most productive.

It is the extension of this paradigm of 'I' that manifests itself as paradigms of profession, political ideology, ethnic identity, and even the attachment to previous work practices in the workplace.

Hence the ability to become aware of the paradigm that is present is a pre-requisite to go beyond such limitations and to move ahead. Becoming aware of the operative paradigm itself creates a certain degree of freedom to think and identify the limitations paused by the paradigms.

Once you become aware you can apply different techniques to go beyond the limitations. This awareness comes when you are able to observe what goes in your mind as it is. This is a skill that can be developed at an individual level and can be institutionalized in organisations as a methodology to practice yielding better results.

18

Is your identity intact?

Recently I saw an advertisement for a paper shredder calling it an Identity Theft Buster. Identity theft is a big issue in the world now – a new risk as a result of the technological advances.

But what in fact is identity? When we are born we are given a name by our parents. In different cultures there are different traditions. In certain societies naming has remained constant over the years, whereas in some countries the names have moved with cultural trends and changes. Although it was given to us by others our name is so precious to us. We are very particular how the name is spelt and pronounced. When the name doesn't sound right, we even get it changed.

The name is only one part of our identity. As much as identity is given to us by others or the outside world there is a process that goes inside us as well that make us link with this identity. This linking or the identification by ourselves with these external props provided to us is the sum total of our identity.

Physical form and capabilities are a predominant aspect of our identity. Some are very happy and proud of this identity and some are not happy about the way they are. Sometimes when the external images that are portrayed as ideal are different to one's own form then there is a conflict and this leads to unhappiness. The identity of the physical form can be even on one or two aspects of the whole body like hair, height, complexion, features and teeth etc.

We build our identity around what we can do with our body. The things that we know as well as our memory are other significant aspects of our identity. In fact, memory is the biggest anchor of self-identity. If we lose our memory then there is a major crisis about our identity.

At a deeper level our identity is linked to what we know, experiences, thoughts, beliefs and even sense. All our mental formations and thought manifestations form and condition our identity. As we grow older some of the faculties fail to function as they used to when we were young. This retardation affects one's identity. Some feel miserable because of this. That is why some elderly hate to wear hearing aids, or use walking support unless these are absolutely essential

The immediate implication of this identity about self is the ability to compare ourselves with others in relation to those identity dimensions. This is such a habitual conditioning it happens automatically even without thinking of it. Our attitude towards the other person will depend on this identification that compares one with the other. The outcome of this comparison is deciding whether one is superior, inferior or comparable with the other person. This comparison is the basis for many human relationships whether they are positive or negative.

What we possess can condition our perception of our identity. Branded products give us a status that can be expressed easily.

When we look at this whole phenomenon by taking a step away from it, it is easy to realize that almost all our activities and experiences are either linked to our identity or impact the process of strengthening this identity.

Ask a hard question, what control do we have over these processes really? Isn't it paradoxical to realize that we have little control over any of those as much as we want them to. Once one discovers and realizes this reality there is a sense of freedom that helps to manage moments when things go in ways that are not desirable. When things do not happen the way we expect, if we know the true nature of this process then we can operate in a simpler light-hearted manner. Such people are unaffected by the changes in the external circumstances that have negative impact on their identity – a quality true leaders possess. To comprehend this aspect of life not intellectually but empirically one needs to spend some time observing how the mind works with some distance, a skill that can be acquired by constant practice. The practice of developing mindfulness to become aware of what happens in the present moment.

19

Check the meter before the crash

'Power' is a word with many meanings depending on the context in which it is used. Whether it is a person's or organsation's strength or ability, or whether it is the power of an engine or in the context of mathematics, power communicates something positive; it connotes strength or an ability.

The word 'power' is mostly linked to the ability or the strength one or an organization has over another person or institute. For the purpose of this article I shall consider the feeling of power when one has power over resources or people.

The other day, I addressed over two thousand persons during a company event. I could command the whole crowd. I felt a sense of having power. The following day I got really sick after contracting a viral flue. I could barely pick up the phone and speak. I felt so powerless. The two contrasting experiences made me reflect upon the feeling of being powerful.

If we take the simple definition of 'power' as the ability to influence a group or a process or decide allocation of resources that is what we experience as power in the context of the business organization.

Somehow, 'I feel the need to have power', seems a basic human need for when some people feel absolutely powerless or helpless they feel like committing suicide. Indeed some do commit suicide. Some act completely irrationally when they lose power. Loss of power has devastating effects on people.

We gain power through many sources. Some are external like the wealth we have, the social net worth we have, the positions we hold, etc. and some come from personal sources such as charisma, physical strength, knowledge, particular skills and so on.

The moment we realize that we have a certain degree of power, we identify ourselves with this state without our knowledge. It happens so quickly and we begin to feel it as so intrinsic, and permanent, that it is very much a part of ourselves. We completely forget the source of power and in the final analysis all these sources of power are essentially beyond our control. Take a very personal intrinsic source of power like memory or knowledge about a subject. It takes only a few seconds for a blood vessel to rupture and the brain to be damaged losing all that strength. Any other external sources of power, of course, can leave us even faster. Yet we do not feel the impermanent side of power and we think it is something that is there forever.

This feeling always gives us a basis to measure and compare with ourselves. As long as we feel superior, we feel confident and comfortable. The moment this measurement gives a negative score, the behaviour changes and sometimes it can be very dangerous as well.

There is nothing wrong about power. But the concern is what happens to us and our behaviour when we realize we have power. Power is an important ingredient of survival of the species as well as the society. But the effect it can have on the individual sometimes or most of the time can be a bit disturbing. Hence the need to manage the effect that power has on the individual. In an organization, power is given to individuals who hold certain positions to deliver results as per the objectives of the organization. But it is very interesting how we forget the purpose of power but try to be possessed by power and protecting the power base becomes the main pre-occupation. This losing of track then causes the organization to fail. Hence it pays to take a step backwards and check the speedometer. Otherwise, we will end up driving using the power and forgetting the journey and when a crash happens the car and the driver both sustain injuries. To know how power affects us, we should develop the ability to look at ourselves objectively. This certainly is a skill that can be developed.

20

Respect and Recognition – handle with care

Respect and recognition is perhaps one of the most fundamental needs of the human being. All religions teach the need to respect every human being while some teachings such as Buddhism and Jainism extend this to all living beings. It is so intrinsic to our survival we take it for granted that every one of us must get our due respect and recognition. Respect and recognition from the external world also influence our purpose and meaning for life. Otherwise, our very survival is threatened, we feel!

Respect and recognition means how others relate to us. Though there is a distinct difference between the genuine respect and recognition a person extends and the artificial recognition and respect extended because it is either the 'done thing' or is done with an ulterior motive. However, this recognition also has somewhat an intoxicating effect on the individual. That is why even this artificial respect is valued by some and their behaviour becomes very sensitive to this recognition. However short lived, some thrive on it as it gives them meaning.

In the past people were respected primarily for *who* they are based on family background and such social standings. Then it evolved to be *what* they are with society seeing more professionals etc. Lately it has moved to become what one possesses, hence the use of expensive branded products as a means to demand respect and recognition. By associating with such brands internally one feels the satisfaction that it gives, recognition and respect he or she desires. Similarly having identified this innate need for recognition globally there are organizations that present recognition titles and rewards to people even for money. Because there is a perceived value to the receiver of such recognition.

Most of these recognitions are given to us by the external world. However much we love them we need to know that they can also go away for some reason or the other. In Nazi concentration camps they used to remove every single possession of the captives. By shaving their head and body hair, not only the recognition or respect was removed, even the identity was taken away. According to most accounts this had been even more painful to them than the physical harassment, according to records.

Without our knowledge we build and augment our own identity and how we perceive ourselves using these external props given to us in the form of recognition and rewards. There is nothing wrong about it. After all that gives us a very good feeling and in many cases we richly deserve such recognition and reward. But we need to know the temporary nature of these. It is like the comforts in a hotel. The moment you check out of the hotel all that is gone. A person who has a very high respect and regard in the village may not get it the moment he or she moves to the city. Some of our local identities and recognitions are of absolutely no use when we step out of the country. We read stories of how even world famous people have not been recognized in certain situations to their dismay. This goes to show what little control we have over the identity we build around or build using the recognitions and respects we get from external sources. So the trick is not to say 'no' to such recognitions which is not always possible, but to be aware of their transient nature and not get too much carried away by them so that it is not a heavy load on us. This is a very important attitude to those who move into leadership positions in any sphere. While those who thrive on such recognition are a lot to deal with, those who take them lightly are a treat to live with.

Enjoy all the recognition and respect but knowing very well that you have no control over them so that when they are not there you have lost nothing.

Reflections:-

Think of five ways how the ideas discussed can be relevant to you

1)..

2)..

3)..

4)..

5)..

Living with others

21

'When I feel smaller'

Jealousy is a common human feeling. It is such a common occurrence yet we hardly take time to explore it rather than saying it is bad to be jealous. How can we do something about it unless we know exactly what jealousy is.

As discussed in a previous chapter, we build our identity by taking into account all our physical, psychological and material belongings. The self image thus created becomes the centre of all our thinking and activities. It naturally lends itself to the process of measuring, comparing ourselves with others. This comparison permeates in all aspects of our lives. We compare ourselves with others in terms of our physical conditions, our abilities, our material as well as intellectual possessions such as qualifications, knowledge, health conditions, social status, standards of behavior, and even feelings. In all these comparisons we usually like to feel better than the other person. Whenever we feel smaller in any of these dimensions then we feel bad, we feel sad. It becomes a state that is not comfortable, simply we do not like the status. For instance, remember the time when you were sick as a kid? While you were sick and confined to bed or you were indoors how did you feel when you saw your siblings playing outside? You felt agitated for they were having more fun than you.

This type of comparison is possible and common with people who are closer to you. Not only in terms of physical or relationship proximity but in terms of relevance proximity as well. For instance, take the peers who work with you and those who are in the same profession. In comparison if you feel smaller than the other person it can cause a little irritation in the mind. This can be the beginning of the process of manifestation of jealousy. It is a reaction to the inability to accept the fact that the other person is enjoying a better position than you in relation to what aspect that is being compared with.

When you think about it, it is impossible not to feel jealous about another person one time or another. The real challenge then is to realize how it emanates and influences our thoughts and actions. When we feel jealous in reacting to a situation, we need to manage the responses. In order to do that we need to be sensitive to observe what goes on in our mind and this is a skill that can be developed. Once we become aware of the presence of this uncomfortable thought or feeling we can work on it rather than letting that feeling significantly influence our behavior.

22

Is appreciation a skill?

From our childhood we are told that jealousy is bad and many stories are related to illustrate how cruel people have been to others because of jealousy. The fairy tales like Snow White are nothing but plots developed on the human tendency of jealousy. But I feel we discuss very little of the antidote for jealousy, or the opposite of jealousy. It is known as "Unselfish Joy" – the ability to rejoice at the success of the other person.

It is said that parents can feel proud and happy and can rejoice when their children do well but not when others do well. And the feeling of unselfish joy is described as the feeling parents get when they see their children do well. The question is can we feel exactly the same when my peer or my relative or even a sibling does better than me, without making me feel smaller than him. Here is the root cause for the arising of the feeling of jealousy.

Most of us do not like to look at blood. But even those who could not look at blood as children, if and when they enter the medical college and become doctors they develop the ability to look at blood which becomes a routine operation for them. Even those who jump from heights or take physically challenging sports don't do them with ease on the first day itself. They develop that ability over a period of time through constant practice. Hence we call it a skill.

But it does not mean that they do not have the tendency of being scared of such situations. What happens is that they develop a mental ability to be otherwise. Developing the skill of being able to rejoice at the success of another person falls within the ambit of such abilities or skills. If we consider anything as a skill then there must be a way to develop that ability. Of course, there can be tendencies that some people can develop such abilities easier than the others. But in principle skills are universal and can be developed but it is the mastery or the performance that varies.

We have seen how those who do well help those who are less privileged and when the recipients do well they feel very happy about it. The question then is can a person who is not doing well also develop the same kind of positive thoughts? The answer is "Yes" if one starts developing such thoughts as a skill.

This is a process of conditioning the mind by programming it to act in a particular way. Every time when one sees another person doing better in life, if one can develop the practice of wishing that person well, congratulating that person even if it does not come naturally or wholeheartedly it is a good beginning. You begin to admire the positives and successes of the other person. It may not be easy at the beginning but one can start by learning to tell oneself, "He is doing well and I am happy about it." Then he can continue developing the practice of complementing the others when they do well. Sending an SMS or an e mail or even a card can be the next level of developing the skill of unselfish joy. Going further, sending flowers or a similar gift can be even better. So if one constantly conditions one's mind to learn to say, "I am happy when you do well" and get inspired by that success then it generates a very strong positive mental energy that is far more pleasant than feeling jealous. If this is developed by more and more people, the whole society will take a positive path of celebrating each other, than trying ways to bring down those who are doing well. At the end of the day if we accept the ability to rejoice at the other person's success as a skill then we can develop this skill resulting in a happier life.

23

Who made me unhappy?

We relate to the external world through our senses. The moment a stimuli hits a sense organ a complex process takes place within the human system. It happens so fast we hardly realize that it has so many steps. The first step is the sense organ coming in contact with the object. For instance, the light rays reflected on the surface of an object reach the retina and generates the signal that the eye can see. This immediately gives rise to the process of realizing and recognizing what is seen. To recognize what is seen, the memory compares the present picture with the past pictures that are stored in the memory. If it is similar to an image that is stored in the memory we say we recognize the object and give it a name. The name is very important for the mind to feel comfortable.

From childhood we always sought names for the objects and all the experiences we had. Remember how we asked our parents for names of every little object that we noticed in the environment? As we grow, the names acquire more meanings through experiences and knowledge. These extra associations tend to form opinions, likes and dislikes about the experiences. It is not the external object that creates these likes and dislikes but these associations that we build around the experiences. That is why, same objects are perceived differently by different people. Even the same person will have different feelings towards the same stimuli, for instance the same bell that rings to begin the school, when, rings at the end of the day makes students much happier at that time.

Most of the time we become happy or unhappy based on these external phenomena because of the way we value, judge or interpret them. There is nothing good or bad about it but that is how the way our mind works. But the question is, should it be like that always or can our happiness be independent from these external situations? Do we think it is possible to be happy in spite of external stimuli at all? If we can be happy independently of these, can happiness be a part of our life and can we be happy always? These are questions worth exploring using our own lives individually.

Are we willing to do such an exploration? Or do we think that the present state of affairs where we become happy and unhappy based on the external things is acceptable? Will a movement from the present to a neutral stage be a boring lifeless stage? These are questions one may want to deliberate using one's own experiences.

Instead of allowing the external world to be the cause for our happiness or unhappiness, can we take responsibility for a situation realizing that the present state is a consequence of our own projections to the situation that has caused the present feeling? Can we be in command of the situation, at least in situations that we are unhappy? In situations of being happy, too, it is a much more stable situation if we can remember the conditions that have caused the happy feeling. Then we do not go overboard with the feeling of being happy as well.

Becoming aware of these processes alone can be beneficial even if total mastering of the situations may not be achieved. Once we become aware of the present feeling then we can create some space between the feeling and our reaction towards it. This provides a good base for healthy relationships at work as well as at home. Then instead of saying you made me unhappy or angry we can realize that the expectations we had projected onto you have caused this feeling because your actions did not match my expectations.

24

Plug and play Friendships

In life persons we associate closely, can be categorized into two broad groups – friends and relatives. Our association with these two groups is described as friendship and relationship. This is worth closer exploration. We cannot choose relatives but we can select friends. The moment we are born we have a set of relatives. In certain cultures relationships are very important. This is signified by the specific words that are available to precisely describe what the relationship is.

One unique feature of relationships is that they essentially depend on duties and obligations. Parties in a relationship have to fulfil the expectations of either party to keep the relationship going. The moment these obligations are not fulfilled the relationship can come to an end or it can be severely strained. This is the position with relatives of the family and all the relationships we have in work life as well.

On the other hand, friendships are bonds we build with persons who, in most instances, we meet accidently. In friendships we agree to accept each other as we are. We have nothing to hide with our true friends. Friendships are not based on duties and obligations but on the joy of knowing each other for whatever reason. There is so much happiness generated when we are with true friends. They remain friends even when one is more successful than the other.

Success in the fields of education, profession, career, economy or wealth has no significance in a friendship. Friendships are so special, so much so that we compare well maintained relationships as friendship. So the expression "in our family we are more like friends".

In business the partnerships we develop are called business relationships but not *business friendships* because in business such associations are and must be based on obligations and expectations.

Although there can be friendships developed among the people who engage in business transactions, the fundamental basis is a relationship that is governed by rights and obligations. Nevertheless it is even empirically proven that the performance of employees is better when there are strong friendships among them.

It is, however, important to distinguish the two types of associations lest they are strained due to misunderstandings. This happens when friendships are developed among partners of business relationships and when business relationships are developed between friends. It is a very thin line and if this is not understood properly the result can be very painful.

In business relationships, however strong the friendship can be, it is important to be upfront and clear about expectations of either party, especially in cultures where saving face is considered important. In such cultures partners avoid discussing the burning issues early enough to avoid or even to resolve. Eventually they end up very bitter.

Marriage is another example where friendships end up as a relationship. Once married it is no more a friendship but a very strong relationship both emotionally and legally. There are explicit as well as implicit expectations, rights and obligations of either party. In every strained marriage the root cause is this kind of unfulfilled expectation.

If relationships are to be maintained both parties must constantly be focused on the basis on which the relationship is developed and continue fulfilling those expectations.

In a true friendship there is no such obligation. When such friends meet even after many years the friendship flourishes from the point they lost touch with each other. Even if there was a disagreement true friends will know how to resolve them. Such bonds are like welded gold; without any marks, whereas a clay pot if repaired the mark can be seen. True friends are difficult to find though.

Good friends are those who are there with you not because of "what you are" but "who you are". It is not easy though to recognize true friends. Sometimes a crisis in life gives us the opportunity to recognize who our true friends are and in that context such difficulties are worth that much more in getting the opportunity to know who a true friend is.

It is worth reflecting on the following quotation about friends by Richard Bach.

"Don't be dismayed at goodbyes, a farewell is necessary before you can meet again and meeting again, after moments or lifetimes, is certain for those who are friends."

***

In a very popular teaching of Buddha known as *Sigalovada Sutta* he has described the following unique description about different friends.

"Young man, be aware of these four enemies disguised as friends: the taker, the talker, the flatterer, and the reckless companion.

"The taker can be identified by four things: by only taking, asking for a lot while giving little, performing duty out of fear, and offering service in order to gain something.

"The talker can be identified by four things: by reminding of past generosity, promising future generosity, mouthing empty words of kindness, and protesting personal misfortune when called on to help.

"The flatterer can be identified by four things: by supporting both bad and good behavior indiscriminately, praising you to your face, and putting you down behind your back.

"The reckless companion can be identified by four things: by accompanying you in drinking, roaming around at night, partying, and gambling."

"Young man, be aware of these four good-hearted friends: the helper, the friend who endures in good times and bad, the mentor, and the compassionate friend.

"The helper can be identified by four things: by protecting you when you are vulnerable, and likewise your wealth, being a refuge when you are afraid, and in various tasks providing double what is requested.

"The enduring friend can be identified by four things: by telling you secrets, guarding your own secrets closely, not abandoning you in misfortune, and even dying for you.

"The mentor can be identified by four things: by restraining you from wrongdoing, guiding you towards good actions, telling you what you ought to know, and showing you the path to heaven.

"The compassionate friend can be identified by four things: by not rejoicing in your misfortune, delighting in your good fortune, preventing others from speaking ill of you, and encouraging others who praise your good qualities."

25

Diary and the family

After attending the funeral of a friend of mine we sat in his living room with his family members recalling the memories we had about him. During this discussion his 30-year old son said, "My father and I lived in two different worlds. I cannot remember a single day that we played together. About five years ago I told him so when he and I were walking one evening. Then he asked me whether I really missed him not playing with us. I said 'yes' and there was a deep silence between us for a long time, in fact until the walk was over. At that time I was in my final stages in the university doing my IT degree. A few weeks later my father bought a computer for himself and started learning to use it. He was sixty-five years of age at that time and he started discussing his computer problems with me, then on. I thought that is how he tried to make good for the childhood play time we missed."

As you can imagine there was a deafening silence in the living room and I saw some wiping their tears.

I remember my childhood days. Every evening my father would tell me a story and chant *pirith* (Buddhist stanzas of protection) for me to go to bed. Thankfully there was no electricity until I was seven years and the other amenities that came along with, so we had time to listen to stories, to go to the paddy fields in the evening to watch the cloud formations, admire the sunsets over the paddy fields, and the moon rising over the hills. Some nights my father (he was a teacher) would take the black board out and draw the constellations of stars to help me observe the night sky.

During the last two decades we have seen a vast change. One thing is certain. This speed of change will be faster every year with the advancement of technology and the commercial activities. We used to travel in buses with our friends, which was great fun. We have begun seeing people, particularly the youth, with earphones listening to the same song over and over again very often being alone in the crowd missing human interaction with the fellow passenger.

We have increased the frequency of communication with our loved ones but may not be at the same depth that it used to be. See what happens when an aircraft lands. Every one pulls their mobile phones out, switches them on and makes a quick call "we just landed and will be out in a few minutes". The anxiety of receiving a letter from a loved one, someone who lives in a faraway place is no more. Thanks to Skype even if the family members are in the four corners of the world, seeing them and speaking to them is only a click away. Rarely do we get surprise visitors for it is not practical and not necessary. In offices people are so busy staring at the computer responding to e-mails thinking and perhaps implying that they are working. Those days the mail reaches you once or at the most twice a day and there was enough time to prioritize and attend to them.

What happens to the time that we are supposed to have gained with all these improvements? We have become so busy that we take our loved ones for granted. I have seen many who have discovered creative ways to beat this shortcoming using the same paradigm of busy-ness that we are caught in.

They fit in a week day lunch with the family members, meet the children after school before they go home or for extra activities at a place the kids like to have a snack and engage in a little chat. There are some who get their secretaries to block certain time slots for different members of the family during the week so that it becomes an activity that is fitted in to the total system that drives us. I also have met some who have found structured activities, well planned outings, discussions among family members so that beyond the mundane "what shall we have for dinner tonight", more in-depth discussions take place. Rather than just watching TV by themselves they agree on programmes the whole family can watch together and do that as an event. Such bold and creative diary blocking is essential to ensure that the loved ones, the family members who are the real stakeholders of our lives are taken care of.

26

Which Part of Life?

It is implied that devotees remove their shoes before entering a temple to leave behind worldly thoughts.

Managers expect employees to forget all about home and what happens in between home and office no sooner they swipe the card or sign on the attendance register. But this is hardly possible. Yet we expect this kind of compartmentalization of life in the context of work.

When teachers see students daydream in class they ask them to come back to the present moment. We tell employees to keep their problems at bay and focus on work.

It is worth exploring this whole question of interdependency of various roles we play in life.

From experience we know while engaged in a completely unrelated task how some other issue, a thought or an idea props up.

We also see some people trying to keep their life in water tight compartments saying that their personal life has nothing to do with work life or the professional life. But is that the case?

I feel that life is a combination of all these things. It is like one big rope that has many threads. Intertwining of all these make life. Some may be strong and some may be weak but they support each other. When one or many of those threads are really weak then we say the rope is weak, and it is at such a point the rope breaks.

These different threads in life can be recognized by the many roles we play in life. As one advances in life in terms of responsibilities and age, generally the number of roles we play increase and again reduce if you were to live very long.

In the morning, the role of the driver who takes the kid to the school, the parent who shares love and affection in conversation, takes a complete turnaround the moment he/she hears news item over the car radio that affects the business, the role of the business or profession comes to the forefront. A quick call is given to the office to arrange an urgent meeting, then reverts to the parent-driver role. Once in the office if he happens to be in a senior position, he plays many roles during the day – as a problem solver, resource allocator, strategist, sales person, PR person, motivator, – the list continues. While engrossed with the office work, he will suddenly remember an important task of the family and will either attend to it or will start thinking about it. A quick call to the wife, and come evening he is playing the role of the president of his professional group and joins the others in the gym before going home to take the family to a dinner outing.

While we go through the motions of the day all these roles and their implications are affecting us consciously or unconsciously. Sometimes they affect the different roles we play in different ways.

Each role demands different levels of energy and commitment from us and the positives and negatives of these different roles leave some permanent and some temporary marks in the process we call life.

Once we become aware of this simple reality we begin to approach life differently. Poet Khalil Gibran, in Prophet said; *Who can spread his hours before him, saying, This for God and this for myself; This for my soul and this other for my body.*

Life is one continuum and it is all about how we play the different roles. When a weight is lifted with the help of a pulley different parts of the rope get the pressure at different points. Similarly in life different roles we play at different times exert different pressures depending on the situation. It is worth always trying to be focused at what is at hand now while appreciating the fact that many other demands and effects are in play.

Being aware of the present moment is going to be a critical capability to notice the challenges of the present moment.

27

Paying Forward instead of Paying Back

Dai Ichi Life in Japan sponsors a series of seminars every year organized by a foundation to promote life insurance in Asia. They invite candidates from all key disciplines of life insurance companies in Asia with a fully sponsored package. At these seminars they share the best practices of Dai Ichi Life Insurance without any reservation. I first thought that this must be a long term strategy to understand the markets and their practices for them to enter the markets later. When I attended a programme in 1999 I was told of the thinking behind this project.

Apparently, after World War II, Japan was helped by German Insurance companies to restart the insurance business. They wanted to show their gratitude to those German companies, but the German companies did not need any help as such. Hence they had decided not to *pay back* but to *pay forward*. Having associated with them for twenty years I am convinced of the intention of this project. Let us explore this concept of *"paying forward."*

We usually talk of being grateful and paying back. The whole process of being grateful and remembering the help offered to us by another person is very interesting to observe. As human beings we cannot survive on our own. From the moment we are born till we die we depend on many others in different degrees. Sometimes we don't even know the people who have helped us.

In life we pass many moments where we need help from another person. The intensity of the problem influences the degree to which we remember the help we got. At that moment we genuinely think we will never forget the person and the help he gave. But sometimes with the passage of time we face many other challenges, problems and crises in life and seek help from many others.

At different stages in our lives we face different challenges and problems. Those who help in different situations become very important at those specific moments but a subsequent challenge can overshadow the previous problem. Some of these incidents can be so significant and we remember the persons who help at those moments very well throughout our life but others may get drowned by incidents with greater intensity.

Now on the question of paying back, sometimes the person who helped may not be in need of any help. It is also possible that the original person may not be living or the second person who got help may not be in a position to help.

There are some who very carefully remember the specific persons who help and find ways and means to show their gratitude. There are some who forget those who helped. There are some who may not specifically remember but help when the need arises and of course, there are others who harm those who helped.

Being grateful is a skill that can be developed and can be a way of life – **Living a Life with an Attitude of Gratitude**. On a regular basis if we recall those who helped us either in different stages of our life or in different roles we played in life, we will naturally recall many who helped us in both big and small ways. Obviously, we will not be able to go back and pay gratitude to all of them. But we can feel grateful towards them, at least be thankful to them in our thoughts and do what was done to us, to others. That is 'paying forward.

Reflections:-

Did you find these ideas relevant?
If so what will you do differently from tomorrow?

Define Success

28

The glass is half full

Success is what we always aspire to achieve. On many occasions it becomes the whole purpose of our being. But do we really stop to question what success really is. Is it merely getting what one wants or should it be considered in a much broader context.

One of the prime feelings of being successful is the feeling 'I have'. It is not the feeling of "I have enough, therefore I do not want any more", but the sense of "my having".

To understand this feeling we can explore how we feel the opposite – "I do not have". Then we tend to think small, think very short term, think petty. It is the poor person's thinking pattern. It is how the less confident person thinks. It restricts our imagination, the ability to see the possibilities. Instead we begin to notice the inabilities.

The happier people are those who can feel that they have. They are the kind of people who overcome difficulties. You may have read stories of people who shared their only belongings with the fellow inmates while suffering in concentration camps.

Recently I visited a friend of mine the day before he went through kidney transplant surgery. I also met the donor who was from a much lower income group than my friend. There I met one of the happiest persons I have ever met.

Responding to my question, what made him donate a kidney, he said, "I have two kidneys but I really need only one." I am yet to comprehend the simplicity of his thinking. Later I learnt from the nursing staff that he had shown no pain at all after the surgery which is more complicated than the recipient's.

This is the kind of positive mind that makes one feel "I have" or "I have enough" the feeling of abundance.

When we study the behavior of successful people we can see how they use this feeling of "I have" in their thinking.

They are the entrepreneurs who take calculated risks not from a point of feeling poor but from a feeling of 'having'.

This feeling is a conditioning one can choose to develop instead of the negative or poor person's mentality.

The common saying "is the glass half full or half empty" directs us to this attitude of 'having' instead of 'not having'.

The moment we choose to think "I have" or in other words begin to look at the possibilities of a given situation that gives strength to look at the options from a positive frame of mind then we have a creative mind. A mind of abundance.

A prisoner who uses very simple tools such as a spoon or a nail to dig a passage to escape does that not with an empty or poor mind but with a mind of "I have".

This is a choice we can make at any given situation. The moment you feel that 'you have', you get the strength to move forward in confidence.

The feeling of abundance is linked to the ability to enjoy what one has. There are some who are wealthy but cannot enjoy the benefits of such wealth. Either they are too busy enhancing wealth or are scared to spend it now thinking of the future. At another level if one cannot spend on a need and have no regrets about it then it is considered the ability to enjoy what one has. This joy is linked to the first and the selection of the lifestyle. Happiness of life does not link with the degree of purchasing power or the net worth of the person. At an economic level if a person can manage to do what he has to do with the income he has, then he can be considered happy. This is the link between the lifestyle and the monetary strength of the person. Since no man can have everything it is important to select a life-style and goals that are congruent with it. For instance, just because a friend invested in the latest model of a camera a person should not make it an excuse to invest in such a camera himself unless he, too, has a similar interest in photography. Taking such a pragmatic approach to life ensures the joy of having and the pleasure of enjoying what you have.

Another aspect of success can be freedom from debt. The recent world crisis illustrated just that. But at an individual level getting into unbearable debt is directly linked to the lifestyle of a person. Hence the selection of the lifestyle can be the fundamental to have an attitude of abundance and the ability to enjoy what one has and be able to live a 'debt-free' life.

Underpinning all these is the means by which one earns one's living. If it gives the joy of being free from guilt as to how one has earned the wealth that is the biggest satisfaction one can have. Didn't the recent corporate scandals highlight the importance of this single most important aspect of success.

These four dimensions of success – the joy of 'having', the joy of being able to enjoy what one has, the joy of being free from debt and the joy of the guilt-free feeling about what one has earned – are found in the ancient teachings of Buddha as well.

29

Formula to Fail

I was reflecting upon why I crashed my advanced level examination (equivalent to University Entrance) the first time I sat for it. I could identify five reasons. I started observing these tendencies in myself and always tried to overcome them. Whenever I overcame them I was successful, otherwise I failed. During my numerous training programmes I have asked thousands of participants whether this is true for themselves and the answer was a very convincing YES! Let me share them with you and I would like to know whether you would feel the same. Ever since I discovered these five factors, I have been speaking about them to students at school gatherings on "how to fail exams!" In order to simplify my presentation I developed an acronym called RAPID.

R= Restlessness and remorse – meaning lack of focus, inability to stay on course and being worried about what was done or not done in the past.

A= Aversion – fighting and avoiding situations that I do not like

P= Procrastination – postponing things to be done later

I= Indulgence – giving into the demands to satisfy senses forgetting the task at hand

D= Doubt – lack of self-confidence, not having a clear idea of the path to be followed.

Let me now elaborate how these manifested in my student life.

Restlessness and remorse- Although I entered the Advanced Level class hoping to become a doctor (a profession I still love), when it came to studies I really did not have a focus. I used to sit hoping to study a particular subject only to change the subject in a few hours without completing the lesson I set out to study. I never went to a tuition master continuously. I got easily distracted with other issues that were outside my immediate relevant subjects, including politics. As the date of the examination drew closer thoughts of regret filled my mind building stress.

Aversion- The expression "I hate that subject" was the way I wish to describe my attitude towards the subjects or subject areas that I could not master. I avoided the difficult subjects. I use to lose my temper very often and many a time with my room-mate. He and I argued about how we should be keeping our room clean – absolutely irrelevant to the objective of getting through the exam!

Procrastination- I had very good reasons why something should not be done at a particular moment. I postponed doing certain tutorials at home hoping to do them in class and once I was in the class, I postponed them to be done during the tuition sessions. I kept on postponing and ultimately did not do them. The end result was that there were many questions I had not attempted even after my third shy. Looking back my excuses were flimsy ones – as it was too early in the day, or too late in the day, just after a meal, or was about to eat, before practices, after practices and so on – simply anything to delay..

Indulgence- Having come from the village to the city the new found freedom gave me enough opportunities to go for movies, hang around or visit friends, seeking popularity in school (I spent more time in the cadetting room and later on, in the prefects' room than in the classroom). When the alarm went early in the morning I stopped it and continued to be in bed so when I finally got out of bed, it was quite late. I found studying at the table not so comfortable and discovered that the most comfortable way was to lie on the bed and study, only to find I had fallen asleep!

Doubt- Obviously this type of student life did not lend itself to developing a strong self-confidence in myself. I did not have a clear understanding of what was needed to be effective at the examination. When I sat the examination the first time I did not know the minimum marks I should get to enter the medical college. I discovered some topics of the chemistry and zoology syllabus for the first time at the examination hall!

Later I discovered how these tendencies affect achieving goals set by us in our day to day life and in the world of commerce as well. If we accept that these are human tendencies then as long as we have humans running businesses and organizations these aspects can affect the way we work and it is nothing but natural.

RESTLESSNESS – It is very common to shift from one activity to another without completing what is at hand. The present day work life environment, in fact, has many external factors that thrive on this human tendency. The e-mails, SMSs, and the phone calls can do exactly the same thing. At a more strategic level not being focused on the agreed strategy is very common and some of the decisions and actions we take are completely counter-productive to the agreed strategy. This I see as a result of the presence of restlessness as a human tendency. At the same time it is the remorse that creates so much tension and stress in many ways an executive life.

AVERSION – We say *"kill the messenger"*. This is exactly what we do when aversion is present in our mind in the context of work. In many business situations we do not want to accept the bad news. When the market research says that there is negative perception in the market we ask for more evidence. At the meeting the one who challenges the status quo is not the most popular. We avoid listening to that person..Sometimes we even fight with the clients! We avoid speaking to the difficult clients because of this dislike. At a strategic level we try to fight the competitor rather than the competition by winning the customer. How many ego battles fuel the advertising wars providing only amusement to the public.

PROCRASTINATION – The moment we say "Let us do this next Monday", what we do is delaying the activity by one week without even realizing it. There are many important but not so urgent activities in work life and in the organization. We delay doing these until they become urgent and important thus creating excessive stress. The habit of procrastination is in a way linked to physical sloth as well. At the same time the mind also gets lazy and slows down. If allowed to continue this, too, can become a dominant barrier to success. At a strategic level we take inordinate time to make decisions because of the presence of this tendency.

INDULGENCE – This can expand from individuals indulging in excessive satisfaction of their senses and allowing them to have habits that cost money, time, health and reputation. Other than that, subtle forms of this tendency can drive us to favour those whom we like, to carry on comfortable tasks without moving away from the comfort zone, and to build organization practices physical and otherwise that soothe our personal egos and images. Excessive luxuries can be a result of the presence of this tendency.

DOUBT – This can vary from the lack of self-confidence of the individual to the organization not having a common understanding of the purpose and the path. The common issue of not having a collective understanding of the organizational strategy among the staff is in a way a manifestation of this tendency among individuals.

Actually I could structure these concepts after reflecting upon the five hindrances mentioned in the Buddhist texts. In describing these, the texts provide some very interesting similes. They are, of course, given in the context of spiritual advancement but I think it is quite appropriate even in the mundane situations that we discussed above.

The 5R formula to overcome RAPID

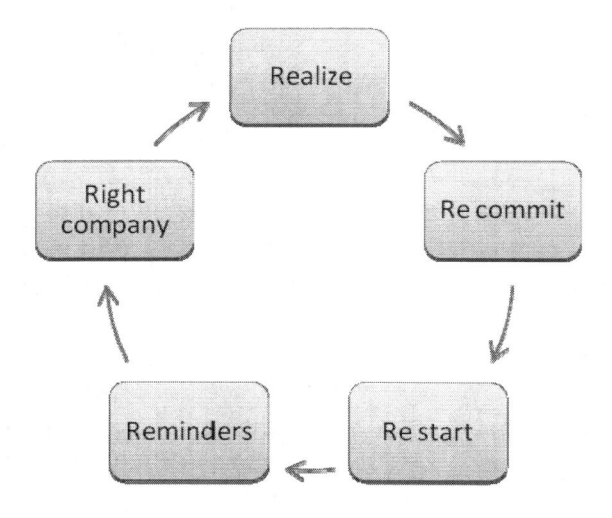

REALIZE – Mindfulness help us to become aware of the fact that we are drifting away from the goal and what factors cause the drift. This is realization.

RE-COMMIT – Since it is nothing but natural for such deviations it is always a good idea to re-commit to the original goal. Haven't we learnt this from many stories told to us early in life? This is a strong mental commitment we can make by reflecting on the positives of achieving the goal and the negatives of not doing so.

RE START – Having re-committed we must re-start the process from the place we have already stopped. At this point it is important writing down exactly what is the first task that will be done towards the goal. It should be so clear we should be able to indicate a Date and a Time to do it. Otherwise it can stay in the realm of wanting to do not in the realm of doing.

REMINDERS – This is a good way to bring us back to the task at hand. These can be words, statements and pictures that can remind us constantly of what we want to achieve or commitments to be made publicly, promises made to loved ones.

RIGHT COMPANY – This is the most important step. Right company or the right association is so critical to achieving goals. What I mean here is not merely regular association with the right kind of persons but more importantly allowing such person's words, deeds and thoughts influence your own actions. In that context they can be words of wisdom found in books, or biographies of successful people.

30

The art of giving

*"All you have shall one day be given;
Therefore give now, that the
season of giving may be yours
and not your inheritors".*

Khalil Gibran

Every religious teaching praises the virtue of giving. At a superficial level giving helps the needy. Giving can be a way to share wealth and by doing that those who have get protected maybe from being robbed. So one can suggest to give for purely selfish reasons.

At another level giving can be done to get more from the recipients on a later date.

Some can give through sympathy and kindness knowing that the other person is less fortunate.

There are other instances where people give to those who may not need but to get the satisfaction or blessings by giving such offerings.

Giving though manifests as a physical activity it is very much a thing of the mind.

To give first you must possess it. When you own something you build a certain relationship with that object.

Without such a relationship you cannot own anything. This is not physical but purely psychological. Sometimes these belongings can even make a part of our identity. For instance the car you drive, the watch you wear can be part of your image, identity. Then giving such items can be very challenging.

A person who was seriously ill thought of preparing his last will. When the lawyer asked who should be the beneficiary, he said to the lawyer; "write my name."

Though, sounds funny isn't it the reality? All material possessions we have exist not out there but in our mind. Just close your eyes and try to recall your most valuable things. They may be in a safety locker of the Bank but can't you see them in your mind's eye. If an object that you love a lot is damaged or lost where do you feel the pain, you touched it, felt it, but in your mind. The challenge of giving is giving up this mental relationship to the objects or our possessions.

Even after presenting a gift how much we like to see them used. Don't we like to see the glow in the recipient's eyes when they open the gift. That is because even a gift though we present it has a link to our mind.

If that relationship is severed then it really doesn't matter what the recipient would do with it. Real giving is letting go of all those attachments. Such giving is indeed a skill that has to be developed by giving regularly and becoming aware of the psychological attachments that have to be overcome before during and even after giving. Then we can give and forget. As the Holy Bible says, the left hand need not know what the right hand is giving.

Giving is a very good practice to become aware about our own limitations and how we relate to things. Being sensitive to the process of giving will bring us face to face with our own likes, dislikes and prejudices. That is why some compare giving to a battle.

31

Prisoners of Food

Consuming food is such a normal habitual routine and our attention is mostly given to the taste, appearance, and related health concerns and issues. Actually come to think of it there are two groups of people who need and who do worry about food. They are on either ends of the spectrum. At one end are those who are extremely poor and those who are affected by disaster who are uncertain of the next meal. To those who live in such conditions, the thoughts about food can predominate their mind for it is a matter of life and death. There is another group of people who also have to think about food quite a lot but not in the same way. They are those who are rich who can afford any amount of food but they may not have the time to enjoy food when they are hungry for they are too busy earning. Then there are the others who are affected by certain health conditions linked to food. Such people, though they could afford it, hardly get a chance to eat, sometimes not even their favourite food item because of medical advice.

During the days of Buddha there was a king named Kosala. We are told that he was an obese person who used to eat a lot. It is said that he used to eat one quarter basketful (half a bushel) of rice and meat curry! As one would expect he found it very difficult to sit still after eating such a lot of food.

The King had a habit of visiting the Buddha at least once a day. On one occasion because of his other commitments the only time he could come to see the Buddha was immediately after a heavy lunch. Though he came he found it very difficult to sit still in front of the blessed one.

The Buddha asked the King what was wrong with him. He very politely said that this was the normal difficulty he had after every meal.

Then the Buddha asked him whether he would like to get some medicine for this condition, to which the King responded positively.

The Buddha then called a minister and asked him to remember the following stanza.

"the stupid one, when he is torpid, gluttonous, sleepy, rolls about lying like a great hog nourished on pig-wash, goes to rebirth again and again". (Dhamma pada- 325)

He was asked to be by the King when he took his meals, and to recite this stanza just before he took the last mouthful.

Whenever this was done the King would stop eating further. The minister was advised to reduce that much of food from the next meal and continue to do so until he reduced his portion to a normal person's diet.

Having practiced this for some time without much effort the King changed his dietary habits and managed his health.

Isn't this a very simple dietary instruction that is valid even today? Aren't we advised to eat in moderation if we are to maintain good health?

Man is the only animal who eats for reasons beyond hunger. In addition to being hungry we eat, because it is the time to eat, to please others, through habit, because we love a particular food, we also eat to try it out. It is good if we can become aware of the main reason as to why we eat every time. That alone will be a good enough practice towards better health. After all it is widely accepted that food is one of the biggest killers of the modern day.

32

Examination before the lesson

A friend of mine was suffering from regular headaches. His answer was to take a painkiller and get back to work until he collapsed one day. The family had to rush him to hospital and he was diagnosed with brain cancer which was in a pretty advanced stage. He survived a few years with medication.

Once when I was suffering from a headache I asked for a paracetamol from an European friend who was with me and she said, *"This tablet represents our modern civilization"*. Elaborating further she said a headache is only a symptom and not an ailment. Most of the time it is the body's way of saying *"time to take a break."* But we are so busy with what we consider is important and do not take a break. We gulp a tablet and continue until it becomes unbearable and sometimes beyond recovery. The person is sick or dead without even completing the so-called important things. Yet the world carries on.

I do not intend discussing the link headaches have with physical ailments for which I am not at all competent. But the point I want to raise is that we tend to follow the same behaviour whenever we are confronted with true challenges of life.

In life when we are confronted with many stressful situations we tend to approach them by way of solving the problem in ways that are easy and superficial instead of confronting the core of the issue. It is easy to take a drink, listen to some relaxing music, or take a walk, or have fun with friends when we are really stressed out. This is similar to taking a pill to suppress the symptom. Even the solutions we give are mostly at the level of eliminating the symptoms from arising for a longer period. But if we go and face the inner issue that causes stress then we emerge having learnt, with greater wisdom about life that is sustainable.

For instance, when we are faced with fear of uncertainties, we tend to look elsewhere instead of trying to understand the true source of the feeling. If we start observing the physical manifestations when there is stress that is something real and gives us a feeling how the stress is affecting. Being gentle to oneself on the feelings and still going deeper to understand where the fear is coming from will give us greater insights as to what life is all about. This kind of insights will lead us to understand that we are expecting certainty from things or conditions that are fundamentally uncertain. Once that kind of insight is reached by direct observation it becomes true life learning. Thereafter one approaches it from a different level of confidence. This is like a father who knows that the balloon with which the child is playing can burst at any time. When it happens though the child begins to cry, the father would say "Don't cry child, we will get another balloon," for he knows that balloons burst. But this understanding does not prevent him enjoying playing with it, admiring it. Getting deeper realizations of life is what is expected from us at every encounter we make in life. In life the test comes first and the lesson later, unlike in the school. Hence it is important to know when we are asked to take tests in life. Taking a pill is avoiding the test and missing the lesson.

Back to the work place

33

Responsibility and Accountability

We cannot speak of responsibility without speaking of accountability as well. Accountability is a word that is mentioned very much these days in the context of governance and management.

Responsibility refers to the delivery of obligations and duties. It is doing what is expected from a person. Fulfilling duties is the bare minimum. In a work situation one can be pulled up for not being responsible since it is what is expected.

Some take responsibility lightly while some others take it very seriously. It is important to examine why this difference in behaviour occurs. To understand, it is important to explore the thought processes that take place when one is given a responsibility. When the responsibility is linked to an undertaking there are consequences to the person, to others, to the organization, to a piece of equipment, for a process, if the responsibility is not fulfilled in the given manner. In such situations when the person has an emotional attachment to the process or the result then that bonding is the thought that drives responsible behaviour. This can be partly instinctive in the sense that we have to be responsible as a creature. For instance, it is natural for a mother to feel responsible towards the child's wellbeing when the child is very small and growing up. It might be this natural maternal instinct that manifests as more responsible behaviour from female workers at the workplace. On the other hand, can being responsible be an attitude developed over the years as a person grows up from childhood?

I do not have any empirical evidence but would like to suggest that if one learns as a child that there are consequences, if certain actions are taken or not taken- such learning can influence a person to be more responsible. For instance, a child who feared being punished for not doing homework or who ran the risk of failing in a class if the third term test is not done well, then such experiences would teach the child the result of not being responsible. If that is what the child has learnt during the school days then once the person entered the working life we can expect such a person to demonstrate responsible behaviour.

Yet how can we instill a sense of accountability that is something that goes beyond the responsibility. I have heard many elderly persons like grandmothers tell playful children not to do dangerous things for they cannot afford to replace a child if something were to happen to the little one. To me this feeling is the closest manifestation of what is expected of being accountable. This feeling is closer to personal values more than any acquired learning. Accountability ensures that the intended result is delivered. That is certainly going beyond completing the task at hand. Wanting to be accountable is more a moral and spiritual feeling rather than a legal undertaking. It is a motive that comes from character, the inner being of the person. Does this mean to instill a sense of accountability one has to undergo more than the usual education? Or is it linked to the instilling of values in early childhood?

Those who demonstrate the behaviour of accountability do that in whatever the situations they are confronted with. Therefore, it can be assumed as a personality trait or a pattern. How can then this be done?

If one as a child heard stories like that of the *little child who tried to stop a leak from a dam by sticking his thumb* in it, then such stories can influence the child to think that a good person goes beyond the obvious delivery of responsibility.

It is also possible that by observing the behaviour of leaders the others learn to be accountable. When leaders act with a sense of accountability such actions are more powerful than all the verbal communications.

Looking at accountability from another perspective one wonders whether it is part of character. Those with very high integrity can be expected to act with accountability. Integrity refers to a higher order behaviour where one's actions are in total congruence with words. This gives the possibility of being able to predict future behaviour. People with integrity will act the same whether in public or in private. Such a person is accountable naturally.

A person with high integrity always listens to the inner voice. Being accountable then becomes the natural behaviour of the person. The more sensitive a person is to the inner voice, the greater the chance of acting with accountability.

At the end of the day it is a mental skill to become aware of what is happening within you and around you. Hence it is a skill that can be developed.

34

Trust as an instinct

In a village everyone gathered at the place of worship to pray for rain. One child had come with an umbrella. That was an extremely strong display of trust and confidence. This ability to trust is an absolute necessity to survive. We need to have some degree of trust in our ability and in the others with whom we interact and various systems we depend upon. In all these situations there is the underlying uncertainty because the only certain thing is change. Yet we continue to trust and carry on – otherwise we cannot survive.

In one episode of the TV series *Kungfu* two novice monks set out on a jungle path pushing a cart full of produce to be taken to the market. At a junction with two roads they ask a stranger for directions, not knowing that this man is a member of a gang of robbers. He showed them the road that passes the point where the other robbers are and as planned, the two monks got robbed. They returned to the temple and related the story to the teacher. He asked what the two young monks learned from the incident. One said "I learnt never to trust strangers" while the other said "Always expect the unexpected". The latter was praised by the teacher saying that it is the correct lesson to learn.

Trusting is an instinct, an instinct that helps our very survival – hence very subjective. Sometimes the trust is affected by the circumstances we are in. During a very helpless situation one would trust things that are not normally even considered. Past experiences have a significant influence in what we trust and what we do not. At the point of trusting what we have is expectation of a future condition. We expect the future state to be something that we desire. It is so we feel confident and we continue to trust. Sometimes with the repetition of this cycle of expectation and delivery the trust gets strengthened. The stronger the trust the expectation for things to happen in the same way is higher and at the same time the impact of disappointment when things do not happen in the expected is even higher.

Even in business relationships creating trust probably is the easiest stage. Delivering on that trust is the challenge in every relationship. Relationships like this are built only on trust. Trust gives predictability and that is a basis to continue with the relationship.

When the trust is broken more than the material damage or loss, the impact is more psychological. Because of the previous actions and words we build a certain image about the other person, sometimes without the knowledge of the other person. In many instances this image and the expectations are projections of our own imaginations, hopes and wishes. One should not be surprised even if the other person is ignorant about such expectations and images created in our own minds. Disappointment comes when the reality is far from the expectation or the mental image we have created about the other person. When there is a discrepancy we feel let down. This is a very difficult feeling to experience because it is like seeing the destruction of our own creation. It is very much a part of oneself – hence this difficult feeling. It is a feeling of absolute self-pity for you cannot undo the past other than blaming yourself for the decision taken in the past. It is a natural feeling the need to assign blame to another person. When this is possible the person gets some relief. But in this instance when you cannot do that the feeling is unbearable. Hence the gravity of breaking trust.

As much as we need to be mindful of the possibility of being let down when we trust, it is even more important to be sensitive to the responsibility we undertake when we allow the other person to trust us. The first aspect reduces the possibility or the degree with which we get disappointed and hurt and the second makes us more trustworthy individuals.

35

Will you worship the computer?

Before starting work, a traditional Sri Lankan farmer or a craftsman would bring his palms together and pay respect to the tools or to the workplace. Even the housewife does the same after keeping the pot of rice on the hearth. During the traditional New Year (in April) they pay respect to the well, and kitchen utensils before using them for the New Year. From the time he plants the paddy a farmer pays respect at regular intervals until it reaches the plate as rice. They would do it with the same mindset that they have when engaged in worshiping at the temple. In the past, students were asked to worship the books before using them and also after studying. If a book was dropped he had to always pick it up and worship.

Most careful drivers do the same before starting to drive. I have also seen operators in factories doing the same before starting the machine and after stopping them at the end of the day – obviously the continuation of the practice started during the agrarian era.

This simple gesture has a very deep meaning. It recognizes the interdependency of the tool, environment and the man. The act of worshiping or paying respect to an object has nothing to do with the external object. It is what goes on in the person's mind that matters. What is important is the value the person gives to the object and the thoughts that get generated during the process. It reflects the relationship one has with the object, or the place. If something helps the person to live, and if living is the most important thing, then isn't the object that helps worthy of veneration? The important point is the relationship with the external object or the process.

Recently a top businessman related to me how one of his employees looks after the machine he uses. According to him, usually the life span of those machines is three to four years but the machine used by this particular employee is now on its eighth year. The only reason he attributed to this was the manner in which the particular employee uses and looks after the machine. We see this with vehicles too.

Japan is a leader in automobile production, yet I have seen how drivers wipe cars with dusters made out of feathers, removing small stones stuck in between the tyre grooves. All this is with a sense of care and concern. Even in Japan this attitude must have been influenced by tradition that can be observed in the practice of Zen where meditators bow to everything before using. In another Japanese Buddhist tradition the monk bows down to the giver as well. During the traditional Tea ceremony those who take part respect each other for the potential each one has to become an enlightened one.

I explored these observations to raise the question whether this kind of an attitude towards objects we use is relevant to the modern day and age where things are made to throw away not because they are bad but because the new one is better.

Yet even for that short period if we build a relationship of respect with the material world we depend on, will it not make a difference not necessarily to the object but definitely to the user? Will it eventually contribute to productivity, quality and lower costs, which are very important economic benefits?

On the other hand, doesn't the lack of such an attitude of respect, appreciating the interdependency, contribute to the environmental disasters we are experiencing today?

36

Deciding to decide

Managers are always expected to make decisions. They are mostly "yes" or "no" decisions. In the final analysis decision-making is a process where we make a choice of available options. Not deciding is also a decision since it is the decision to delay the decision. Or the choice from the options Do I Decide NOW or LATER?

It is always expected that decisions are followed by consequences. The situation is always different once the decision is made. Peter Drucker recommends that we record our decisions, and the expected outcomes and compare them with the actual outcomes to learn from the decisions, since this process gives an opportunity for us to look at the decisions objectively.

Prior to making decisions we go through a mental process of information gathering and evaluation depending on the expected consequences. There can be a certain level of anxiety depending on the decision and the intensity of that anxiety is directly related to the consequences.

In principle, we like to make independent decisions, but consciously or unconsciously, our decisions are influenced by external factors. There are four main factors that can influence decision-making. They are extreme preference or likeness, extreme hatred or dislike, fear of consequences, and not having the right understanding of the issues at hand or being ill-informed.

All these hinder making unbiased, principle centered decisions. Extreme preference can blur all the negative things about a person or a condition. Generally we like situations where there is approval of our own views, and persons who like us. For instance, this bias can colour hiring decisions, resource allocation decisions, and even delegation decisions in work life. It is not to say it is always bad but it is important to be aware of the presence of this bias so that one can then take an objective view of the situation.

Extreme dislike or hatred is the complete opposite of the previously mentioned bias of likeness and that, too, clouds looking at a situation as it really is. Hatred or dislike prevents us seeing any positives of the situation, in an idea or a person. This mental state of hatred comes when there is a major conflict of views. Here again what is required is to become aware of the presence of hatred or dislike when one is about to make a decision. Dislike, hatred, or anger is such a powerful motive it can push the person to take a decision that can be extreme very quickly without even thinking of consequences.

Fear is the other interesting influence that distorts the mind in making decisions. Fear is linked to possible consequences in the future. When future consequences are considered unfavorable, that influences decision, In many situations, decisions are delayed because of the fear of consequences or decisions against conscience are taken under fear. This can be challenging in certain situations, where one makes a decision to resolve the existing situation knowing very well that the decision is made under fear. Unlike the other two conditions the presence of this influence is obvious and clear to the person.

The final bias is lack of clarity of the situation or not having a proper view of the situation. In reality it may not be possible to have all the information needed to make a decision, and if the limitation is known, then to that degree, the decision can be guided.

Whether in personal or professional life, being aware of these extreme influences, when making decisions can steer a person to make better decisions.

Whatever the decision, the moment a decision is made the outcome is a change in the situation.

In Summary

Ability to become aware of what goes on in your mind will give you the ability to be in charge and to choose your response.

This is a skill that can be developed

To develop this skill, learn to bring the attention to the present moment. For that choose some of your routine activities to be done slower than normal when possible.

Choose the most suitable practice from the many suggested in the book.

My personal favourites are becoming aware of breath and learning to walk paying attention to walking.

Make bringing your mind to the present moment a part of your life. In fact once you start this practice this will become the norm.

This ability to become aware will help you look at yourself objectively thus giving you an opportunity to learn more about yourself, and how you interact with others.

You will begin to enjoy a degree of inner calm, and you will be more stable facing life situations, consequently you will be more effective in whatever you do.

37

Post script

In the foregoing pages I tried to share with you how you can develop this simple yet very useful skill of being aware of the present moment by being mindful and the kind of insights you, too, can derive for yourself.

I have been practicing these over the last thirty years and found them to be very useful in leading a simple life with very few complications.

Do write to me to share your thoughts and if you want me to facilitate executive retreats to develop mindfulness as an executive capability for your organization.

Good Luck with your journey.